FAMILIES ARE FOREVER:
Communication

DENNIS COGSWELL
MSW, Ed.D.

Strategic Book Publishing and Rights Co.

2013

Strategic Book Publishing and Rights Co.
12620 FM 1960, Suite A4-507
Houston TX 77065
www.sbpra.com

Published by Strategic Book Publishing and Rights Co.

ISBN: 978-1-62516-829-0
Library of Congress number: 2013943540

This content is intended to inform and educate and is not a replacement for medical evaluation, advice, diagnosis or treatment by a healthcare professional.

Dedication

My Parents, Robert and Hazel Cogswell

"Dad, I Learned Much and I am Still Learning."

*   *   *

Our Three Grown Children:

Kristen Cogswell, Lauren Cogswell Ramseur and Drew Cogswell

"Every Day We Learn Something From You."

*   *   *

Acknowledgements

It takes a large, extended family to write, publish and distribute a book today. Many different individuals provided much support, guidance and content in the writing of the book.

- Nancy Cogswell, "Nana" in the book, editor, idea developer; life-long wife and co-author.

- Charles "Hobs" Hobgood, The Forever Family Philosopher; Family Consultant; deep thinker.

- Dr. Hal Gillespie, MD. Mentor, Author of Foreword, Friend, Spirituality Leader.

- Dr. David Cousert, Research Director, Family Therapist, Good friend.

- Deborah Brown, Final Editor Supreme.

- Jennifer Spooner, Graphic Artist for Cover.

- New River Valley Writing Project.

- Ms. Jenny McNeely, MSW Original "Kelly."

- Rick Lander, Initial Editor, Good Friend.

- Roger Bell, Bonus Chapter Author as Sir Roger. Financial advisor, & family dynamics advisor.

- Dr. Bruce Mahin, EBook Consultant and Audio Consultant.

- Many 'Beta' Readers.

- Countless others, extended family members and friends who have guided me through the publishing process and shared their family experiences that told me what I needed to know.

TABLE OF CONTENTS

Foreword

News alerts of the Boston Marathon bombings jolted my concentration as I started to write this Foreword. With relief, I learned of the safety of Dr. Cogswell's daughter and son-in-law, who had crossed the finish line, only a few lifesaving minutes prior to the blast. The bombers were identified quite quickly but it was much later that cable television news mentioned the possibility of radical Muslim involvement, although it was known the family emigrated from Chechnya, which is primarily Muslim influenced. The press also delayed posing questions about the family, their dynamics and how these brothers were being supported in a wealthy community. Eventually both issues were addressed and it became obvious that the immediate family of origin had values that were divergent from our culture and had failed to assimilate. It is concerning that the media could speculate endlessly about possible motives without focusing on the importance of family and values, particularly if they involved religion, whether Christian or Muslim. Could the media's stance be explained by political correctness and contemporary cultural beliefs that values do not matter and one belief system is just as valid as another? Do we not as parents need to examine and test our beliefs and then thoroughly and clearly communicate them to our children and grandchildren, while still supporting their differentiation? Should we not be able to defend our chosen forms of Christianity and Islam in intellectual and moral perspectives? Dr. Cogswell does dare to address the issues of values and family communication in the second volume of this series.

Families are forever . . . or are they? The statement may be "true" in the sense that our primary family experiences determine our subjective experiences throughout our lives. We may live out our lives on opposite sides of the world from our families of origin, but the family is still within us even if we are engaged rebelliously against it. Dr. Murray Bowen, a pioneer family therapist, stated:

1

"Maturation is the process of disentangling oneself emotionally from the craziness of one's family of origin without giving up the family." He defined "craziness" as anything that doesn't work for you and your life. But, is this taken too literally in our modern world? Has differentiation become a process of rejection and alienation as children become more influenced by social networking and communication technology? Are parents failing to impart values, respect and discipline? A common experience is to see a family eating dinner in a restaurant in silence, as each member is preoccupied with I pads, cell phones or game boys. Even couples can be noted texting or play electronic games on their smart phones during public concerts and plays. Dr. Cogswell does acknowledge that social media and networking may distort or even prevent family interactions and complicate the process of differentiation. It is hard to differentiate from someone when you don't know who they are. It is not clear how to develop effective communication under these circumstances. The answers may come from someone who grows up in the "wired generation", who understands the phenomenon from their experience. Regardless of how it evolves, communication remains essential to individualization and differentiation.

Families may be forever, but family forms or structure may not be forever. Other pioneering family therapists, such as Salvador Minuchin and Carl Whitaker taught that children are most likely to imitate the behaviors of their parents. Is that observation less valid for the twenty first century? With increasing longevity, more families consist of three generations. The traditional, two parent, married heterosexual households are much less common. With the advent of numerous new constant stimuli for children are they more likely to choose behaviors and values from outside the family? If so, the first challenge for the behavioral sciences is to discover how to enable parents to communicate with their children in ways that teach important positive values. Dr. Cogswell outlines current approaches developed in recent decades to help traditional families. This is a good place to begin the discussion. The resulting question is how traditional approaches will need to be modified for our time. Another challenge, for all of us, is to identify and delineate values that are generally approved across our culture and then encourage their expression in the media, entertainment industry, and newer technological advances.

Utopia may be unattainable; families have always encountered problems and will continue to face problems. In one of civilization's oldest historical accounts, the book of **Genesis,** there is recorded jealousies, deceptions, betrayals, conflicts, and even fratricide in families. Perhaps these ancient myths also contain principles and wisdom that still apply to families today. It has been said that as Adam and Eve were leaving the Garden of Eden, one said to the other: "My dear, we are living in troubled and changing times."

When we examine our experiences of life, it appears that the only reality is our subjective one. We live in a world where our sensory experiences are projected onto the screens of our minds through filters of cultural beliefs, values we are taught and the influence of life events and relationships. This seems to determine one's own reality. With this basic condition, we tend to project this personal vision onto others. Only through communication can the family and the individual members correct these distortions.

No family is perfect. No parent, spouse or child is completely who we want them to be. A major developmental task for each of us is to recognize our own projected neediness and to forgive family members for not being everything we want them to be. In this process we come to love them for being who they are. Perhaps this is the best opportunity in life to imitate God; it's the godliness within us.

In these books, Dr. Cogswell shares his experience and knowledge derived from decades of teaching and working with families. His efforts are applauded as he takes on the challenge of translating theory into everyday language and experience for the nonprofessional reader. He is a beloved friend and colleague and to use the well-worn cliché: he is like a brother to me. It was a privilege to write this Foreword. I certainly do not agree with everything that he says or with all the ways he may approach an issue. In the end, however, we remain engaged in active and respectful dialogue and in close relationship. Is that not what "families are forever" all about?

Dr. Hal Gillespie. M.D.
Spokane, Washington
May 2013

Chapter One

Introduction: Communication in Families

Anyone who has never made a mistake
has never tried anything new.

Dr. Albert Einstein

I wake up every morning and grab the morning paper.
Then I look at the obituary page. If my name is not on it,
I get up.

Benjamin Franklin

This book is about you. It has to be. You are always in a family and that doesn't change. You are born into a family of origin[1] until emancipated around age eighteen. Then you automatically become a member of an extended family that lasts until you leave this earth. We are writing about you. We will share what has been shared by many ordinary persons in ordinary families.

In America today we have a complex medical system that interfaces with all aspects of our lives. Our medical system is driven by money and the profit margin. To get money from insurance companies that fund vast portions of the medical system, we receive a medical diagnosis or label with a number. Being an old system, that label is negatively worded and focuses on what is wrong. It tells us that we have erred, done things wrong and that we

---

[1] We all begin in our family of origin or our birth family. In our Western cultures we traditionally launch our offspring to a more if not totally independent status around the age of eighteen, after they have graduated from high school. They primarily go to college, into the military or get their first job. Most move to independent living.

have a problem. Luckily that system is adjusting and the Forever Family doesn't see things that way at all.

Our two main families, The Forever Family and the Bearister Family represent a "cup is half full," strength perspective, family unity first. The family stories shared comes from people you meet every day in the grocery store, in church, and at the soccer game. They are not problem families but families with hurdles. Family members you will meet include Uncle Charlie, who caused over $30,000 in damages at the local fast food restaurant with his five iron; Aunt Sarah, who sold her husband's and her home and Mercedes Benz without his knowing it, put the money in fifty and hundred dollar bills in two paper grocery bags, and then rode the Greyhound Bus from Vermont to Colorado; and finally, Char, the twenty-year-old college student who has his mother call him each morning to get him up for class. They are life and lively.

However, they are not media driven, so you learn more about them than you would if we wrote sound bites. They are not super heroes so they don't fly nor do they often save the world. They are not what many agents and editors are hoping will populate this book, much as a television drama or video game thrives upon. Alas, we don't give door prizes or points.

We have several websites related to our books: www. TheFamilyForever.com; www.TheFamilyForever.info; www. SquireBinForever.com; and www.BearleyBear.com that utilize multiple media such as YouTube and podcasts. There you can play a round of golf at the world's only underground course, visit an Author's Writing place, Nana's Nook in the Deli for great recipes, read the full bonus chapter sections and visit the Video Screening Room, all of interest to families.

To support you in your normal and typical American family, many experts have been directly consulted or their works read. The bibliography for each chapter is found in an ending Works

Cited and Recommended Other Sources section at the end of the book. Some of the chapters have specific book lists that pertain specifically to the suggestions offered. Some of the main themes of the book come from family system's models, business team building approaches, multiple psychologies and even spirituality models. The recipes base comes from the entire series of _____ *for Dummies*, Lencioni's *The Five Dysfunctions of a Team: A Leadership Fable,* Dr. *Burn's Feeling Good: The New Mood Therapies,* Becvar's *Family Therapy: A Systematic Integration* and such diverse resources as The New Testament and The Kabbalah. It all comes together where readers are offered recipes[2] rather than technical jargon, and well-grounded, researched data and recipes are presented in a very enjoyable and engaging style.

As authors we have enjoyed taking the thoughts of other authors, yours and our life experiences and blending them into recipes that are tried and tested. We hope that we have kept the recipes clear so you can use what you want. My grandfather Claude always told me to follow the rule "Keep your recipes separate even if they both end up at the same meal."

In writing the book, we discovered the following that might be of interest to you:

- It is unknown as to when families began being mentioned in the writings of scholars. Early monks were forbidden to write about families and related matters as that was God's work; however they likely did so but in secret. Doing so

---

2   All that is offered in these books are offered for information purposes. Ideas as to what to do are offered as "a suggestion"; there are always alternative ways to approach hurdles. What is presented is not a substitute for medical or other professional assessment and service offered. On our website: www.TheFamilyForever.com is information on what professionals work with families and how to find one. Use that information as it becomes useful to you.

in secret or public didn't start until our present form of writing was invented in 3200 BC in ancient Sumer from a highly functioning, professionally-based civilization that had priests, professionals, governors, trading people, and artisans providing services;

• The United States Census Bureau estimates that in 2010 there were approximately one hundred fifteen million persons between the ages of thirty-five and sixty-five, the age when most parents head extended families (U.S. Census Bureau, 2010);

• Eighty million of those thirty-five to seventy-year-old parents actually had adult children somewhere in this country. There are another thirty-five million in that thirty–sixty age range who don't have children but almost all are active as an aunt or uncle to a sibling's adult children (U.S. Census Bureau, 2010);

• A focus of this book is the communication between parents and their eighteen to forty years old offspring, often known as adult children. This cohort group makes up thirty-three percent of the United States population (U.S. Census Bureau, 2010);

• Many persons focus on the primary or nuclear family whose children are ages one week to eighteen years. Yet it is the extended families where one spends the most time in life; thirty to fifty years on average. Seventy percent of children in the US live in traditional two-parent families with sixty-six percent of those living with parents who are married and sixty percent living with their biological parents (U.S. Census Bureau, 2010);

- Another statistic states that as of the year 2000, nuclear families with the original biological parents constituted roughly twenty four percent of American households, down greatly from the forty percent in 1970 (U.S. Census Bureau, 2010).

As this book is about you, here is a sample of the questions that you have already asked us. We have responded to each question with one answer, although there could be many more. In the book, many more vignettes are shared. As always, the stories are true as fact is better than fiction; they are carefully disguised. When people read these examples, they often say to themselves: "how did you know to write about me?" Even we, the authors. asked the question about ourselves: "how did we make it as an example in our own book?"

- **My husband and I argue a lot and end up blaming each other and saying some ugly things to each other. I know I have fifty percent of the blame here, but so does my husband. How can we get out of the cycle?**

  This is often a dilemma that extended family parents experience. All of the books have something for you on this issue. I think you will get the most from Book Two: "Families Are Forever: Feelings, Those Rascals." In Book One, read about changing in general and changing feelings specifically. I think you will find what you are seeking.

- **I feel guilty a lot of the time. I am a quiet guy and don't usually say much but recently have opened up to others. However my friends tell me that I am very judgmental and that they don't like that new part of me. Neither do I. what do I do?**

This is a common situation and can be remedied with a little work on your part, starting with changing a few words in your vocabulary. In addition to reading in this book about changing feelings, do some reading on your own about judging and feeling. If you have a religious background, talking with a minister you trust might help. See the chapters in this book on communication and in Book Three: "Families are Forever: Family Relationships" that would be of value to you.

- I am fifty-four and my adult kids are finishing up college and onto their own lives. I still do things for them but the time with them keeps getting reduced and I certainly don't get anything back from them. I seem to have a lot of friends who enjoy my company but only when I ask them; they never call me and ask me to do anything with them. I think I am happily married, going on 37 years but my husband is very busy with work and his golf and bowling leagues. What can I do to feel better about myself and make my life better for others?

We want you to set a goal of making life better for yourself first. You need to continue helping others but only when you have negotiated something you want back from what you give. You will still do a lot of helping others but from a position of negotiation rather than 100% giving. All three books have much for you. In this book the chapter on assertive communication will be of interest to you. It is now "ok" for you to begin sentences with the pronoun "I". That will feel funny at first; It will be an important step in reaching your goal.

- I am thirty-eight year old mother with twin twenty year old community college freshman. They are living at home until they can transfer to four year colleges in their sophomore years. We have always been a close family but having two-live-at-home college students is now a real challenge to that unity. We do have conflict that we haven't had before and my husband really runs from any controversy, even when I talk to him alone about it. He goes to the upstairs den and watches TV or down to the basement to make tie flies for fishing. I need his support and parenting help. What do I do?

Your husband is going to his Man's Cave to get away from the arguments; read the second chapter of this book to get a handle on that. Then read about extended families. Extended families are the foci of all the books so all will have information for you. Remember that feelings are always involved. If your sons happen to be taking an Intro to Psychology college class, they might be interested in these books as well.

- Our only son is 29 years old with an accounting degree from a well-known university. He has held a couple of jobs and lost them all each time the company downsized considerably as he had little seniority. After his second job loss, he moved back home to his old bedroom where he now has lived for 4 months. He does little but play video games and goes out with friends occasionally. He has no present goals, and does not really look for a job. We want him out of our house and back employed but do not know what to do?

Book Three, "Families Are Forever: Families Relationships" has an entire chapter on the Boomerang Generation and several chapters on Parent & Adult Child Relationships. However, the other two books have considerable information that you could use to work with you husband on this common but tough situation. Whatever you decide to do, it must be presented as being a joint wife-husband decision.

Author's History

For many reasons, I am very sure that "Families Are Forever". When cave person's writings were discovered, they came from a family grouping and have ever since records have been kept. I have been in a family for the sixty some years with no ending in sight. I started out in my family of origin or nuclear family that consisted of my father Robert, mother Hazel, and younger brother Roger, all deceased. It is quite sobering to be the only living member of that family after having my own nuclear family,[3] I am now in my extended family that numbers in the dozens, depending on how you count. I spend almost every day with my wife of four decades, Nancy or Nana. We have three grown children: Kristen, Lauren and Andrew, and have five grandchildren. All of my adult offspring are happily married. There are many aunts and uncles, nephews and nieces, cousins and more. We have family friends all over the United States who may be counted as extended family. I start by being an active Christian in God's family, and belong to many organizations and groups. They have changed over the years with some always being constant.

The books, *Families Are Forever: A Trilogy* came about for several reasons. One was the importance of families to Nancy and me. I love to learn and I had never written a book for the general public although I have done much technical and professional writing. I have learned five new software programs and read forty books new to me to accomplish this as writing a book in the twenty-first century is much more than putting pen to paper.

---

[3] It is interesting that most books on families are written on the nuclear family even though you are a member for only about eighteen years, It extends from age eighteen until your death; as long as sixty years for some. Little information exists here although this family type is the biggest and longest in duration. The extended family has many forms and variations.

The book's focus is communication, feelings and relationships in extended families. It was influenced by research my colleague Dr. David Cousert did on Emerging Adult Children and their Parents (Cousert, 2011). We discovered that little was written on extended families, those families with adults other than parents over age eighteen. Thus I set out to do change that!

As the lead author in a narrative book, I share what I have learned from others. You will hear directly from me and through the five main characters whose voice I type into written word: Dr. D., Kelly, Squire Bin Forever, and Vincent and Lucy, our fifteen year old contributors. I have a Doctorate in Adult Education and a Masters in Social Work (MSW). I will share my experience as a family counselor, trainer/educator of new counselors, and father of adult children and grandfather (Papa) of five grandchildren. When I am not here writing my books, or in The Forever Family Complex, I like to ride my bike, garden, play golf and the card game Bridge, and build things. I love to learn and enjoy the process more than the outcome."

Nancy Cogswell is an active co-author and chief editor. She proof reads the material written by everyone and co-authors at least one chapter in each book. If asked, she says: "I am Nancy or Nana, known lovingly as Nana to my four grandchildren. I write from that name as well . . . I have been married to Dennis for so long, I can't imagine not being married to him. I set aside my nursing career to work from home until our first child went to college. I then went back to work as a Public Health Nurse where I worked with families and young adults around their pregnancies, young babies/children and also in relationship to infectious diseases in the community. I like to spend my non-writing time in gardening, bird watching, biking and with my grandchildren, family and friends."

It is time to learn more. Select either a paperback or electronic version of this book. Don't forget the website www. thefamilyforever.com as it changes weekly. There are free downloads of the first chapters of each book, Table of Contents and links to other sites there. In order for any change to take place, some muscles have to be moved, so now is the time to move some muscles and go to your next destination. Remember, there is always more to learn

© Dr. D.'s Domains 2013

Chapter Two

Listening, Hearing and Doing

*The test of whether you are a thinker or not is whether you go
to the ocean by yourself and preach or listen.*

My wife thinks I say too much.
Probably.

Dr. Dennis Cogswell

More Than Expected

Dr. D. was in a very good mood as he walked down the path to
the Forever Family Complex, his home away from home deep in
the Colorado Mountains. He and others had used it for years while
he worked as a professor of family counseling at a nearby major
Colorado university. Last evening was a great evening for him.
He guessed it was the same for the others. At least that was what
Nana, his wife and co-author, said to him as they said their final
goodnights. Their discussion last night about today's extended
family was very important. Hobs shared how he was doing deep
thinking about our adult offspring, our adult children's generation.
He said that a significant portion of this generation holds a very
different set of beliefs about the nature of the relationship between
them and their parents than any other generation. This generation
seems to have less interest in connecting with their parents in
sharing their lives and utilizing their parents' experience e.g.
the need to hold the same political beliefs, or to go to the same
church. Family customs are not anywhere near as strong, nor do
they maintain the same level of family contact. These offspring are
inflexible on this even though they state that they are open to and
value differentness and change.

It was good to discuss new things and Dr. D. was sure tonight's post-supper get together would continue the discussion of this topic. How fast the months had gone by since his retirement. He had finally adjusted to not teaching or counseling, being free to travel, doing special things with Nana and the two of them with Kelly. He liked looking at the photos of his five grandchildren and the ultrasound picture that he carried in he carried in his wallet of the fifth grandchild before his birth. Now, he often can do things with and for them.

Inside a huge and tall 10,000-foot-high mountain, the Forever Family Complex had grown immensely. It soon will be one of the stops on The University's Monorail system. It has seven floors to it with guests and staff entering at portal six and then going up/down to anyone of the other floors via the elevator system, depending upon their designation. As a portion of a higher education learning system, the Forever Family Complex's University Hall has a library, classrooms, conference rooms, a video and audio viewing room, an observatory tied into the Hubble Telescope system, the world's only underground golf course and a large outside viewing deck. If you like birds, bring your binoculars as people are spending time watching two Great Horn Owls raise their latest two offspring. How appropriate for a place that focuses on families.

Dr. D. pushed the button to the floor where his office was located along with the offices of Nana, his wife of four decades, and Kelly, the thirty-five-year-old Master's Degree in Social Work (MSW) counselor who had joined them as a project advisor several years ago. Once inside the elevator and alone, he began sharing his thoughts out loud to the four walls. "What Nana and I found so attractive about Kelly was her work with families that she had carried out in a church-sponsored family counseling agency close by in the Colorado mountains. Then, what really made us offer to have her become a permanent member of the team was her personal positive energy, commitment to the values of the Forever Family of being proactive, interested in strengths, looking for win-win recipes, seeking family unity, and valuing parental influence rather than control. We knew she would contribute much to the Forever Families' concept. What we didn't know is how much fun she would be." The walls said nothing so he took that to mean agreement.

The elevator seemed to be taking forever to get there. Dr. D. was shocked when the door opened and the hallway was full of men and women, all in their forties and fifties. Most of them gave him that blank elevator look. The door closed and off they went. "Hmmm," Dr. D. mused. "Wonder where they came from? Perhaps on a misguided tour from the Visitor's Center. Oh well, maybe it is a new guide. The experienced ones know that the staff floor is off limits. I will soon be to my office where I can quietly sort books, read the latest on blogs and enjoy myself. Maybe Kelly will be in with some of that good coffee for that she is famous."

He finally got an elevator by himself and went down to the staff floor. He was surprised as the hall towards the conference room was crowded with the same people he had seen before. He had to fight his way to his office and was about to enter when he saw Kelly going into the conference room with two pots of coffee held over her head. She didn't see him but seemed to know the others. He tried to work in his office but there was too much noise. As he often did, he talked to one of his leather and wood side chairs: "Guess I might as well go see if I can help Kelly with whatever she has going on." His chairs said nothing, which he took for agreement.

Dr. D. worked his way over to the side of the conference room where Kelly was speaking to the audience. "I enjoyed this morning. I hope what I had to offer met your needs, although what was offered by the keynote speaker did not . . . Oh, here is Dr. D," she said. Much to his surprise, they began to applaud. This he did not expect. What was going on?

Time to Listen

Kelly knew Dr. D. was confused . . . After the applause died down, she said: "As you hoped, here is Father One of The Forever Family complex." That again brought applause. Dr. D. not only didn't know who these people were but he didn't know why they were applauding him.

A familiar figure pushed his way up to where Kelly was standing. He waved to Dr. D., and then to the audience, and got silence. It was John Bearister, Dr. D.'s and Nana's next door neighbor. Now Dr. D. saw Judy Bearister in the front row, waving quietly to him. John spoke clearly, first to the group, and then towards Dr. D. "I know most of you don't know me other than the brief moment when I was introduced as the organization's new president. I am honored to hold that office for the next two years and equally honored to be here at The Complex, the home away from home for Kelly, Nana and Dr. D., my next door neighbors down in the valley. Let's hope Dr. D. will speak to us on the Forever Family approach as it applies to Empty Nesters . . . I am here today with my wife Judy. We have been married for thirty-two years and have three grown children. They are David, Michelle and Ian. As a writer by trade and a columnist for my regional newspaper; I write a total of four columns a week, two each in the areas of money management and computer usage. I have been in this group before as my other two adult offspring went to the University as well, graduated and left the nest. I think that experience and being a member of our group for four previous years suggested that I might have some experience to bring to our discussion. Experience, yes, but answers, no."

John paused and then began to mention last night's conference lead speaker . . ." He never got beyond the speaker's last name before people were talking loudly among each other. One father even shouted out, 'tell that no good speaker of this morning to go home to the East and let them deal with him.'"

There was so much emotion here as if something bad had just happened. That exactly was what happened earlier in the introductory session where Kelly introduced the speaker. The main speaker not only didn't do well, he also was rejected by the audience immediately. His credentials were excellent and he was experienced, but he either misspoke or started off in a manner that he likely will not do again. After only two minutes of a speech, the booing started. Then, he didn't respond directly to his audience and suddenly grabbed his I Pad, coat and stated: "I am out of here; I don't have to take this harassment. You will get my bill for sure." He then left. [4]

Kelly took charge as she had been watching it all back stage. She came out front, took a sip of that coffee she always had, and got the audience to quiet down. "None of us expected this," she said. "Please realize that the past is past and we cannot change or influence it. We have the present, Now, and the future. I know John and the Executive Committee will review his presentation and see if our speaker violated his contract. We have this afternoon to live and let's do it right. I know you will love your trip up Trail Ridge Road to the Sky in the Rocky Mountain National Park[5]. I invite you to stop by The Forever Family Complex on your way back here. I will either talk again with you or Dr. D. will. If he is in then, I will ask him to talk on our view of hurdles all Twenty-first Century families face and what enabling really means.

---

[4] The speaker by using a traditional approach that looks at problems families have. Although it is a well-known and science-based approach, it typically puts listeners in a very negative position and seems to blame. He said: "I hope to address some of the problems you Empty Nesters have been having with your adult offspring. They are typically the result of common mistakes, especially the mistake of 'enabling.' or well-meaning but deadly help. I know some of you are helicopter parents and it is time you give that up and go on with your own lives." He got no further before the audience disapproval started."

[5] Learn about this great road at http://www.nps.gov/romo/planyourvisit/trail_ridge_road.htm

"I know what resulted in your anger. It seemed as if our keynote speaker was going to blame parents for the problems he saw in typical empty nest families today. That definitely is not the way the Forever Family approaches this important topic. We don't see families as being problem families or that parents are to blame. Instead we talk about issues that all families face as a part of lifelong development and how a win-win approach works best. Our views are not unique to us. We take the positive approach to everything and see life as offering opportunities to enjoy and experience much achievement.[6] Yes, there are hurdles, but all families face them.

"I will join you on your bus. The Complex is but a few miles from one of the entrances into the Rocky Mountain National Park. I think the afternoon will be great fun. You will see a beautiful National Park, and hear a talk that relates to your group's focus. Grab your gear, go to lunch and John Bearister will greet you when you get on the bus."

An Overview of Dr. D.'s and Kelly's Mantra, Offered Again.

Some of the key points the Forever Family offers include:

- Although it may seem that parenting is over now that your offspring are adults, the need for parenting goes on forever. What changes is the amount of control a parent has and how they must move from being in control to only 6 (Becvar, 2003), (Dodson, 2011) (Johgeward, 1998), (Lencioni, 2002), (McGraw, 1999), (Minuchin, 1998) plus at least twenty more.being influential. Our new role is one of a supporting and mentoring role;

---

6   (Becvar, 2003), (Dodson, 2011) (Johgeward, 1998), (Lencioni, 2002), (McGraw, 1999), (Minuchin, 1998) plus at least twenty more.

- The parents of adult children have told us repeatedly they want information on what influences their offspring to be the way they are and ideas to consider helping make relationships good one. It is our goal to provide both of these;

- Many parents do seek out the services of a family based professional. If so, find one who will listen to you and other family members about your situation without any blame at all. Seek a counselor to help you make any changes from your strengths. Counselors don't have all the answers and will tell you when they don't know an answer. What they do have is information and ways to go about figuring things out;

- In the Forever Family, the focus is not on problems but instead on the hurdles families will face as they grow and develop. This growth and development is a life-long process;

- Parents and adults in extended families will learn that it is both normal and desirable that each be puzzled at times; that means that they are concerned but not overwhelmed with a strong emotion such as anxiety or anger. They will learn how to release their bad feelings through recipes provided them;

- As the growth and development occurs in the extended family, it will be learned that most understanding comes after moving beyond that which you are trying to figure out;

- The issue resolution process we offer only utilizes a small amount of family history. Our change process begins with "what are your goals"? All approaches eventually have to get to goals or statements about what you want. Once it is clear what you seek for your extended family, then we can move to "how" you go about it, leading to your developing an actual change plan. "When" and "where" come next;

- It is important that all people become very slow to judge, if judging at all. That is because often things are not the way they seem;

- Communication is a key to satisfactory relationships among family members. Work here includes comprehending some of the subtle nuances of human communication;

- We will do what many others leave to chance and that is show how to change a specific feeling rather than just focus on 'what' ought to be changed.

Approaching the Same Subject and Getting It Right

I see that Nana is coming down the hall with Hobs, their family friend. That means something is about to happen. Let's rejoin Dr. D. and Kelly as he finishes his address to the Empty Nesters.

*   *   *

Dr. D. smiled, recognizing that we are now in the room. He then continued. "As we agreed earlier, I have been discussing a few key elements of being an Empty Nester. The last one is the process of enabling. This process has both good and negative elements. When the word enabling first comes up, we all think about helping out, giving of our selves, supporting, and guiding, all important functions that parents have done for years with such positive results. How can someone speak about enabling as something not to do, something to avoid at all costs and then to call it out as a leading cause of family issues between parents and their adult children? It is not because the process just described is wrong nor that we parents are bad persons for doing so. It is that sometimes the timing of all of the above is not right or the need is actually not there. If we miss-time giving of ourselves, we are not at blame. There are many factors that influence whether what one does with an adult offspring is the right or not the right thing. I repeat, 'We are not at blame; we are to be aware.'"

"We want you to ask yourself ask two main questions: Are we needed? Are we to step aside temporarily and let our adult son or daughter experience life without the benefit of our experience?"

Dr. D. continues. "Char is a twenty-year-old adult, male offspring in his sophomore year in college. His mother, Jolene, still calls him every morning to awaken him forty-five minutes before his first class.[7] Jolene knew that she was behaving incorrectly as a parent of an adult child but was too worried that he would flunk out if she didn't. When she called, he got passing grades. The first half of the first semester of his freshman year, she didn't call and he got terrible grades. Thus, after a lot of anxiousness, she started calling . . . She hoped he would mature sometime. We used the term 'helicopter Mom'[8] as it is commonly used term, but we did not use it in such a negative context as today's speaker evidently did. We, later on, speak to the role the father played and how Char, as an adult, had responsibilities for his own education, and lifestyle.

---

[7] You soon will read the more extensive version of this real situation as described in Chapter Seven of this book entitled, *The First and Last Word Issue: Which One Do You Want?* If that additional information is desired now, go to that chapter and read what will be useful and then return here.

[8] It is often used in reference to the female parent who hovers over her adult children and does too many things for the adult child. She is labeled a "helicopter parent", one who means well but turns out adult children who are losers. Our family unity approach recognizes that parents can overly assist their offspring, which does sometimes result in an over dependency.

"Thus enabling can be good or bad. We know that you Empty Nester's struggle with this choice every day. On your way home, share some of those struggles with those around you so you will know that you are not alone. I end by telling you all to continue helicopter hovering; sometimes be right overhead, sometimes a long ways away so you are invisible yet you know what is happening. Sometimes do not leave the copter pad, but let your offspring know you are there in spirit. Godspeed. Remember, there is always more to learn."

The group arose as one, and as humans always seem to expect the worst, Dr. D. was ready for a negative response. However, it was just the opposite. They clapped hard and loud. He waved his return appreciation, gave thumbs up to Kelly, and went back to his office. To his side chair he again spoke. "That went well, as well as a thirty minute talk on the complexities of family life can go. I am glad I could add to their knowledge. I hope that they think about the beautiful Rocky National Park and what an opportunity they have as parents of adult children graduating from a major university." His side chair again said nothing, which he took for agreement.

From Lemons to Lemonade to Limes: Timing is So Important

It is late afternoon of that eventful day. Kelly has asked everyone to meet with her briefly in the conference room. Kelly, Dr. D., Nana and Hobs sat down in the comfortable chairs in the conference room. After a rehash of how it all came about, Kelly turned to Hobs and said, "Sorry that we didn't get very far in our discussion today.

We recognize that all family members have a part in this, such as the male parent, and certainly Char himself. We certainly wouldn't use the term "babying" but would say "over supporting."

Did any of your experiences at the Philadelphia Child Guidance Center or the Cleveland Gestalt Institute prepare you for today?"

Hobs thought, and then said: "I learned a long time ago that everything is related, to never blame and to seek to understand. I believe that everyone who does something in relation to another is doing their best job to have things be good for all. We focus on the family system. Those who focus on the individual have a core value of 'independence' more so than 'interdependence' which carries with it both opportunity and responsibility. I agree with that value, as long as both opportunity and responsibility are recognized. A system's approach does this."[9]

Dr. D. responds to his longtime friend. "Thanks Hobs, we value your thoughts immensely. You are a great fit for this team. Would you consider joining us as a co-author?"

Hobs: "I am honored to be invited to write with you all but know what my priorities are. My wife, Marabeth, and I have had many life experiences including serving as foster parents and raising our two children, who are adult helping professionals themselves. We will enjoy our four grandchildren, develop ourselves in terms of the next step for all of us, and that is to move from a 'Doing' life to a 'Being' life. I would be glad to chat about any of these important elements."

Nana: "Thanks Hobs. As I get to know you, you are really into life. Your energy and commitment helps energize me to say what I never thought I would say. 'I say, let's write!'"

---

[9] This view does not include people under the influence of alcohol or drugs, or at the moment, being quite ill mentally. In those cases, what we know so well about other situations cannot with any certainly be put to use here. Thus the first goal is to end the substance usage or to get the person back to actively living their life, albeit with their hurdles.

Kelly: "I have always seen myself as a counselor. You have taught me how to help people learn in an educational manner, helping them as much as possible. Like Nana, I too say, 'Let's write.'"

Dr. D. "That we are doing this is not a surprise to me as we all have been talking about this for some time. What is a surprise is that we are deciding on this today. I love to do something I have never done before and to learn in the process. I think that will happen with the journey and the relationships being the most important products. I too say, 'Let's write!'"

Dr. D.'s Famous Summary

After high fives, low fives, hooked fingers and other bonding gestures were exchanged, the three of them went to the Deli without Dr. D.; he would join them shortly. He stated out loud. "There always must be a short summary. Such a process increases learning greatly. Remember, there is always more to learn." He turned out the lights and hurried to catch up to his colleagues. That left the side chairs of the conference room to ponder what he had stated. They said nothing for a while, which suggests agreement.

© Dr. D.'s Domains 2013

Chapter Three

The Family Recipe:
A Look at All the Ingredients

Guilt is NOT an emotion; it really isn't!

Anger is almost never justified, nor beneficial.

*We all are always in or related to a family, often more than one.
First from birth to around eighteen years of age; then to an
extended family for the next fifty to seventy years . . . Many have
issues, hurdles, and disconnects to overcome along the way.
All of this is natural.*

Dr. Dennis Cogswell

The Bearister Family Puzzle

The Bearister Family are good people. All the families are that you will read about here. Some struggle more than others. All do their best with the resources that they have to provide their off-spring with a better life and more than they have. Sometimes that works to the detriment of the family and its members. However, it is the American Way.

The Bearister Family is puzzled. It is actually good that John Bearister is puzzled a lot. It shows he cares, is alive, thinking, and wants things to be better. What used to be the best of times is now not so good for all. When John and Judy Bearister first got married at age twenty-three, just out of college, they put off buying their own home, kept the cars that got them through college, didn't have much furniture, and got jobs in their university town which was only one hundred fifty miles away from both sets of parents. This gave them the opportunity to see parents every holiday and some weekends. They delayed having their first child until both were established professionally and had a good sized nest egg in their bank.[10] By age twenty-seven they felt secure enough to start their own family.

They made decisions about spacing out their kids every two years and were able to do just that with David, Michelle, and Ian. All three children were happy family members throughout their first eighteen years of life, but began to change when in college. The oldest two—David and Michelle—did marry after they completed college, which took them six years, including one year off for travel and David switching majors several times. Now David is happily married with three kids of his own. His wife doesn't see much of her own parents, which in turn influences their infrequent connection to John and Judy.

Michelle lived with her husband-to-be while in college against her parents' wishes. Their life was interrupted by an unplanned pregnancy that ended late in her first trimester as a miscarriage, which was traumatic for all. She has not fully recovered from that loss and won't talk about it or whether she will ever want to become pregnant again.

She did finish college. Michelle comes home regularly without her husband since he works weekends as a bartender to help meet expenses. She gets along well with Judy, her Mom, but not quite as well with John, her Dad, who she thinks is just an old jock. She was very distant from her after her failed pregnancy and Michelle's preference to get her recovery information from her friends and the internet rather than from her mom. This is still a sore memory for both.

---

[10]   Banks used to value the regular family member and pay as much as 7% on a CD and 5% on a Savings Account.

Ian is the "pink elephant in the room". Ian sailed right through the first two years of college until the end of his sophomore year when he had to declare a major. Then, things went downhill fast for him. Against John and Judy's advice, he moved in with some new friends, giving up the friends he had lived with for two years in the dorm. However, those new friends did support him financially and emotionally as he struggled on both accounts. As he had to declare a major, he chose liberal studies, a dead-end major job-wise that was there for the few who were undecided. Ian flunked out the middle of his junior year, couldn't get a job, and then showed up on John and Judy's doorstep one evening, announcing he was now a "Boomeranger". He has now lived with his parents for the last twelve months. He shows no sign of moving out and on to his own life. However, he is back in school and is pulling "C's". All know that the Bearisters extensive support of him is not a good idea. Looking back, John and Judy agree that they spoiled him.

The three kids are heavily influenced by their peers. They now manage their lives and relationships in the same ways as their friends do. This generation frequently follows all the information they mine from the Internet. If they can't quickly find it on the Internet, they then ask their friends. Parents are left out of the loop until, from experience, their adult offspring learn to value experience. John and Judy have a strong marriage with the only stress and discord coming when they discuss what to do about their communication and relationships with their kids, especially Ian. Judy has become much more emotional and doesn't understand what is influencing her to have those feelings. She gets angry now at the amount of time John spends in his bowling and golf leagues, something that he didn't do when his kids lived at home. John doesn't understand why Judy won't make Ian obtain at least a part-time job to pay a rent payment. He thinks that Judy may be slipping him twenty dollar bills from her own money.

The Bearister Family remembers the best of times and wonder if good times will come again?

The life experiences and outcomes of the Bearister family are typical for families in this 21st century. They are neither a problem family nor a dysfunctional one. They do have what some people say are hurdles to get over and have misconnected often. They are not flawed, bad, useless, or slackers— words that some apply to individual family members. They are disappointed; sometimes angry; often puzzled. They do not know what "things are the way they are" means. Is this "The New Normal"? Does anything ever change for the better?

John and Judy have read books to get un-puzzled. In their reading, they found mostly books about parenting of young children or adolescents, on relationships and on finding one's spouse. These books were interesting, but the examples did not help either communication or relationships with their adult children nor help them know what to do about their feelings that were always there. They want to change some of their negative feelings and biases but these books just told them "to do it", never told "how". Conflict was new to them. John had some beginning ideas from a work-based conflict management seminar that he wondered if he could use with his own adult kids. John and Judy, and to some extent, David and Michelle, recognized that "families are forever" and want things to change or forever might not come fast enough.

*   *   *

As we often do, we share the stories of other family members. Kelly just went to our conference room to talk with two members of the Upp family, who are here from Georgia. We have their permission to use the discussion for these educational purposes. As we listen in, I suggest that you listen to what the Upp sisters talk about and also note the way that Kelly goes about listening and replying back. It is this style and content that comes from our beliefs. This is what will guide us and this is what you will experience in working with us.

The Upp Family Rings Out

Kelly takes a sip from her coffee and begins. "Today we share the story of two sisters from the Upp family, Belle, aged fifty-four and Charlotte, aged forth-seven. Their younger brother Sevin is a college head coach and off on a soccer recruiting trip for the college team he coaches."

Since Belle is the oldest, she speaks first. "Thank you for seeing us as we just learned about the Forever Family Complex. Charlotte and I are very close, especially now that both our parents are deceased. We both are happily married, with our own nuclear families."

Being a chatterbox, Charlotte doesn't stay quiet long: "I echo everything just shared. We came to talk and to ask a couple of questions. We are both active, successful women back in our home community in Georgia. Yet life there is not a happy one for us. We know that people say we have poor self-identities and do not think highly of our selves. That is half-true because we feel very good about our professional lives, but both of us seem to want to take care of others before we take care of ourselves. People tell us that notion is wrong. We don't see how it could be since we've spent our whole adult lives as professional helpers. What advice can you give us? Tell us something to do to make us whole again."

Belle frowns deeply and it shows. "Yes, I am afraid that when you come right down to it, we are damaged goods. We need help from someone just like we help others."

"Oh dear, I don't like to hear someone call themselves 'damaged goods' as that is not how I see you at all," Kelly says with great feeling: "I will be glad to spend time with you today and to give you some direction. I'll get you started and you can come back again and again.

"I don't really need to know much more now about what is not right for you two because we start with 'what are your goals'? I do not need to hear from you about what many call 'the problem' or 'the issue' that we call 'the need' or 'the want'. We are a step ahead of the other approach. All approaches eventually have to get to goals or statements about what you want. Once it is clear what you seek for your extended family, then we can move to 'how' you could go about it, the actual change plan. What are your thoughts about what you want and how you might go about getting what you want? 'When' and 'where' come next."

Belle again takes the lead. "I want to know why I do so well in directing my daycare school and such a poor job managing my own checkbook. I know what my friends are saying about me and it hurts." She cries a little bit, but as a true Southern Belle would, reassumes her strong but lady-like manner, using a linen handkerchief, something unknown to most women today.

Kelly touches Belle's hand briefly and then removes it. "Belle, I'm sorry you are hurting but not that you cried. That was good, both that you cried and that you cried now, releasing those feelings. Crying is a good tension release, for men and women, although some men would disagree. Not our Dr. D., Hobs, or Sir Roger, some of the other Forever Family men. They know that feelings are to be expressed.

"As far as 'why' you do so well in one area but not others almost no one understands what makes things the way that they are until they change. Then things in the past become much clearer. We, in the Forever Family, seldom use the word 'why' as it brings with it bad vibes and usually is answered unclearly. Instead, we ask 'what', 'how' 'where' and 'when' questions. In summary, the first suggestions or recipes for success include: (1) feel what you feel and move on; and (2) use action words that give you a real chance to figure things out."

Belle now speaks strongly. "I heard the recipes about the two communication steps and look forward to reading many more. We do want to solve our own mess ourselves with some help."

Charlotte looks right at her sister. "Belle, it isn't a mess. That is your internal voice speaking when you talk that way; I have one too and cannot shut it off. What is wrong with us?"

Kelly quickly confirms their 'OKness': "I know this seems bad to you and you want to blame someone or something, so you blame yourselves. Please stop that. It would be unusual if you didn't have an internal voice or two as all humans do have them. What is important is how often they come on, what do they tell you, and have you learned to turn the volume up and down on them? Often those voices are serving as your internal compass and are very important in an emergency when you do not have time to think carefully about things. It is when they are negative voices—telling you what to do—that they're not good. One way to tell is if you find yourself 'shoulding' on yourself or others . . . That is enough recipes for now . . . I want you to tell me some more about what you want things to be like. After we get some plans underway and some change occurs, we can go back into your past and connect some things, although that is something you can do. What we do best here is help you learn to fish, not fish for you."

*   *   *

Nuclear to Extended Families: Birth to 90+

We will leave Kelly to continue with Belle and Charlotte, our two visitors from Georgia. They will talk for a while longer, but we only wanted to have you listen in for a short time so you could get a sense of what we had to offer and how we will do it with our families.

Dr. D. is such an interesting person, as we all are. As he enters his office, he arranges the chairs in the conference room in just the right order, only known to him. As he talks to them, he likes to know which chair he is talking to, as some have more experience with him than others. He does talk to the newer chairs as well because it likes their fresh ideas. Then, he goes to the computer and writes in his weekly blog, read by many. Among other things, he blogs about life at the Forever Family Complex at www. theFamilyForever.com/Wordpress. Here is what he offered:

> On my way in, I counted about two dozen visitors in the Visitor Center. Many are downloading the free chapters or listening to the podcasts. I told them there were new recipes in Nana's Nook in the Deli. Several seemed to know that I was "official". Perhaps it was my Bearley Bear sweatshirt that gave me away. Many wanted to know where the book title came from. I spoke the truth. It is because they are indeed forever.

Then he began to ramble about Nana's Nook, where very good recipes are offered for many of his favorite dishes. We will leave him to his dreaming.

Again, Much More Than Expected

We use two descriptive terms about families, our **nuclear family,** the **family of origin**, or the elementary family (Unknown, Wikipedia, the free encyclopedia, 2012) Everyone is born into a family and lives there or at least relates to it for approximately eighteen years. Next, everyone who leaves home "joins" one or more extended families where membership is automatic but not free. Although people are focused on family member between the ages of zero and eighteen, and their parents, these persons are only together in a nuclear family zero to twenty years. Most parents and their adult children live into their seventies and eighties, so the time spent with each other in an extended family is much, much longer than the times spent in their nuclear family. You can be a one person extended family or be a one hundred person extended family when aunts, uncles, step-sisters, your own children are all included. You can have your own nuclear family when you marry or partner that grows quickly in size when you have your own kids. All nuclear families are short in duration, about 18 years, yet so important to the last sixty+ years of our lives. It will all make sense eventually but not likely now.

The idea of a nuclear family seems straight forward until you realize that what once was called a typical nuclear family, made up of a mom, dad and some number of kids, and may not be the norm today. Our view of what makes up a nuclear family expanded over the last decade to now include:

- Blended nuclear families, which are those families where mom and/or dad have remarried and constitute another nuclear family;

- Three generation extended families with the original parents, their off-spring and the off-spring's children, either living in the same home or separately;

- Single parent families, where because of death, divorce or separation, either mom or dad is left to raise the children;

- Common law families, both intact and those where one partner has moved on;

- Increasingly among Generation X, Y or Z'ers, gay/lesbian families where two people of the same gender cohabitate and raise the children of previous unions;

- Same sex female couples who adopt or even give birth to babies through various artificial fertilization methods;

- Same sex male couples who adopt children so they can have a family;

- Separated/divorced nuclear families where mom and dad become divorced or separated, and one or both remarry or move in with someone.

Using the terms of extended family and nuclear family is easy; however, nothing else about these two types of families is easy or uncomplicated. It is no wonder things get confused for all and conflicts become much more pronounced (Unknown, "Family, Extended" Intern. 1 Encyclopedia of the Social Sciences, 2008).

*   *   *

The Family As Always

How far back in human history have there been families to guide and support us? The team member to answer that question is Hobs; he has been dealing with families longer than any of us.

Hobs is not used to being introduced, but recognize that this has just occurred to him. He looked looks around, and then begins. "In most cultures of the world, the beginning of family history is set in creation myths.[11] The ancient poet Hesiod's second poem **Theology** describes the Greek gods' relationships and family ties . . . In biblical times, men sought to prove their descent from the family of the prophet Moses in order to be accepted into the priesthood . . . Roman families would list everyone in the household under the father's name . . . All the way through history, in all cultures, the family thrives . . . In ancient and medieval times, the ancestor's history guaranteed religious/ secular prestige (Unknown, Wikipedia, the electronic encyclopedia, 2013).

"The organization of the pre-industrial family is similar to the organization of today's family. Post-industrial families became more private, nuclear, and domestic and based on the emotional bonding between husband and wife, and between parents and children. Today's families are based on values, and value conflict and/or feeling conflict is a chief cause of family disunity today, as it always has been (Walsh, 1999). The strength of families is in its values of unity, structure (a family is not democratic, never was, never will be), familiar roles and the ability to adapt, but not abandon itself, in changing times. Extended families are about communication, feelings and relationships.

*   *   *

---

[11] Required reading is Joseph Campbell's **Power of Myth** where he clearly affirmed life as an adventure. He gave up the pursuit of a doctorate and went instead into the woods to read books about the world: anthropology, biology, philosophy, art, history and religious books. His overriding theme is that all of modern life and through our history, we humans and family members have followed the Mythology of the Greeks (Campbell, J. & Moyers, 1988).

Dr. D's. Famous Summary

Hobs, ready to turn things over to another, sees an opportunity to do so, and walks out of the conference room to Dr. D.'s office. Dr. D. has his private office on the left, near the Control Center, although he doesn't spend much time there. He prefers to write in a small conference room close by his office. Nana prefers the right side of the complex and can usually be found around the Deli, again in a small office unmarked. When she can, she goes out into the mountains. Kelly is everywhere, especially if there is a coffee pot. She joins whomever she is writing with at their favorite spot. Right now she is with Dr. D in his office. Acknowledging the wave from Hobs that he was "up", Dr. D. began to summarize: "In our next chapter, we will talk with John and Judy about what people have been asking them. We will respond by describing how things are with extended families, offering ways to improve family life through recipes as we all journey through life. Remember, there is always more to learn."

Chapter Four

Basic Communication Tools:
Shoulds, Buts and More Questioning

I can't imagine a God who rewards and punishes the objects
of his creation and is but a reflection of human frailty.

Never do anything against conscience
even if the state demands it.

Dr. Albert Einstein

An Angry Uncle Charlie

It's hard not to listen in on another person's phone call when it begins like this one did: "Uncle Charlie did what?" John Bearister yelled into Dr. D.'s office telephone. John had let his cell phone run down so he couldn't call out, but a text message from his wife said it was urgent that he call her NOW. He had calmed down enough so his end of the conversation could be heard. "Now Judy, you have this right? Uncle Charlie is in jail for taking his golf clubs and breaking all the glass and the soft drink machines right inside the window . . . What made him do that? Was he drunk? OK . . . I don't believe it one minute that he wasn't drinking . . . It was noon time and he went there for lunch and he just went off when they again screwed his order up . . ."

John listened for a long time to his wife telling him the details. He then hung up, with his last words being . . . "Tell the Sergeant I will be there in an hour to post bail." He sat there looking at Dr. D.

Dr. D. was very surprised since Uncle Charlie was a retired minister . . . He sat quietly and finally with hesitation asked, "Are you all right? Is your Uncle Charlie all right?"

It was quite a while before John looked up from the floor and said, "Yes, we're both OK. Charlie has never been this much in trouble before because of his temper but we knew it was coming. What can be done for him? What do I say when I go and bail him out?"

"Go to the jail and as soon as they will let you see him, go and either hold his hand or give him a big man-hug and tell him he will be all right. Will he admit that he has a huge anger problem?" The good doctor paused to see if John was following him. He was.

"Yes, I think so. The Sergeant let him talk to Judy on the telephone and he was calm. He said to her; 'I have an anger problem; I really have to do something about it now'."

"That's good," was Dr. D. D.'s quiet and reassuring answer. "After some basic talk, ask him, 'Are you aware you have a huge anger problem?' . . . Once you get that admission, praise him for saying so and tell him that he has just taken the first big step towards solving that problem and that is owning it . . . 'I have an anger problem' is such a big statement. As he doesn't have a record, if he goes into counseling, pays for all his damage, plus a big fine, the court will likely hold his 'guilty' plea until he successfully completes counseling."

John nodded, apologized for dumping this on Dr. D., and got up to go to the jail.

Dr. D. rose, took hold of John's shoulder, and said: "John this happens. You will be fine and you can help Uncle Charlie. Go to the jail, call home soon so Judy knows you are helping him, then take Charlie home and you go home. Come back here tomorrow morning and we will talk."

I am Dr. D. and so begins a very normal day at the clinic.

*   *   *

Amy Vanderbilt's Curse

That is the first family situation John brought to his weekly meeting with the good doctor to discuss. It is clear John felt relieved that he got the phone call there rather than where he didn't know anybody. Uncle Charlie's situation clearly was about anger, very inappropriate behavior, and even communication. Charlie will learn during counseling about feelings and anger. He will learn new behaviors to do when he feels an anger attack beginning. He will be taught to control his anger by expressing it appropriately and often. He will learn assertive communication.

Effective human communication is much more than the selection of words. It is about relationships, values, and feelings. A different level of a relationship brings about different types of communication. Today, Kelly and Dr. D. will demonstrate some of the basic ways that people use communication, often with hidden messages. Remember, it is impossible for a human being not to communicate . . . Kelly, it's your turn.

*   *   *

Before speaking, Kelly pauses for a moment, looking at Dr. D. but saying not a word. After what seems like a long pause, but was only seconds, she said: "Good mid-afternoon to all. In this chapter, we cover many aspects of human communication and start with the difficult area of socially correct behavior."

Dr. D., with a big grin on his face, thinking about what had just happened, says, "In doing so, we start out by making sure that we don't write anything that will offend anybody . . ."

"I think the good doctor is saying exactly the opposite of what he thinks!" Kelly responded.

Dr. D. was caught thinking back to his earlier conversation: "You are too quick; that is exactly what I was doing. It is impossible to do and say everything in a pleasing way for everyone. How could you? And yet there is a portion of our population that tries to do that in every relationship."

"I certainly agree. That and diminishing the value of apology by way overusing it are two communication snafus I hear all the time." Kelly pauses to sip on her coffee. "I do want readers to know that this column is not anti-etiquette. Etiquette is the way that society has determined things be done the majority of the time. It lists and endorses social norms. Communication protocols help humans not to have to think through everything that they experience. We are not rebelling or endorsing an 'anything goes' philosophy either. We give people permission to be themselves to meet their own needs without stepping on people's toes. We are working to help people develop to their full potential. That is a difficult task as people differ greatly in the way they go through life . . . But let's work at what we all have in common in relation to some communication basics."

But, It's a But . . . .

"You just demonstrated one when you put the word 'but' in the middle of your sentence," Dr. D. added quietly. "Anytime you use 'but' in a sentence, the 'but' erases anything that is said before the 'but' and the real message comes after the 'but'. That you just acknowledged individual difference is often covered up by our common fallacies. Another example will help."

> Roberto, in his mid-twenties, is interested in dating a new colleague and approaches her: "Joanne, would you like to go to a movie with me tonight?"

Joanne, who doesn't believe that colleagues should date, starts off her polite but avoiding sequence by saying: "I would love to, but I have to do my homework sometime and it looks like tonight is it."

Roberto, who doesn't yet realize he is being rejected, replies: "What about then going out on the weekend; you could work on your project during the day on Saturday and we could go to the big game that night."

Joanne: "'The big game, that sounds like fun but I don't know if I want to get wet if it rains.'

Roberto, "trying" again: "Joanne, if it is the weather that you are worried about, we can go to the movie you have been talking about instead of the game."

Joanne: "I would love to see that movie, but I am afraid I won't get my project done in the afternoon." Roberto finally gets it and with head down, goes back to work.

Now I ask you, what do you think are the odds that Joanne will ever go out with Roberto? She is "butting" him, a passive aggressive way of being polite, leading a guy on when you don't want to date him. It happens all the time.

Kelly is quiet for a moment as she thinks about her first husband and how she often 'butted' him: "I'll start listening for 'buts' and hear the real message then after the 'but.'"

Dr. D. "You will be amazed at what you discover when you look at the forest for the trees."

Kelly: "Passive language does help bring communication confusion. What about people who don't adapt to or try to please others as their top priority all the time, but sometimes speak passively because they think it is the polite way to talk?"

Dr. D. answers directly, and quickly. Not only what he says is important, but he is modeling good communication. "A mild version would be this passive inquiry: 'Would you mind if I stop by this afternoon, I really would enjoy seeing your new kitchen?'" The better, assertive response is: 'I have some time free this afternoon and I would like to see your new kitchen. Would it be ok with you if I came by this afternoon to see it and chat'?'"

"What makes the difference is that the first inquiry uses the phrase 'would you mind,' which asks for the respondent's feelings, not whether the person is available to have company. It deflects from the real question which is: 'Are you available to have company?' There is an assumption here that the kitchen owner wants to show off her kitchen. I think it is an appropriate assumption that she would like to do just that so that question doesn't need to be asked. If by chance, she has just shown it off to two other sets of visitors that day and is tired of doing so, in her response to the assertive question she can say: "Actually this is not a good afternoon for me to have more company; would you be available to come over on Thursday afternoon?"

Be Aware. Be Assertive.

Kelly: "Doesn't one always have to be concerned about the other's feelings? Aren't you telling people they don't have to be polite?"

Dr. D.: "I hear your question-statements and agree. It works out best if one is aware of other's feelings; however, that doesn't mean you have to ask about them every time. The good friend has listening and observing skills and will read the situation to see if s(he) thinks there is something going on with how the other person is feeling. This puts the friend who wants to visit in a thinking mode, not an automatic response mode.

"I can give you a counter example to where someone has negative feelings about having visitors but at the same time would benefit from being visited. Jane is a seventy-two year-old new widow. Her husband died four months ago and she is going through the normal grieving cycle. She tends to feel bad a lot of the time. If one just went on her feelings, she would never do anything or go anywhere because basically life has lost its meaning for her. She needs time to adjust; it hasn't been long enough for that to happen. If you asked just for the way she was feeling today, she would tell you this: 'I don't feel good today.' Her thoughtful friends know that, know about being a widow, are respectful of her feelings. They don't discount her and say: 'Come on Jane, Victor is dead. Move on.' They know that being active, doing things and talking to others will, time by time, visit by visit, help her move on. Therefore their statement-question to Jane is: 'Tell me if you are going to be home this afternoon and will accept me coming by? I want to see your new kitchen and more importantly, see you.' This shares the real caring the friend has and lets her know that she is more important than the new kitchen; a question Jane has been asking herself."

Dr. D. is on a roll and without hardly breathing goes on. "The really adapted people use 'do you mind' as slang and use it all the time. 'Do you mind if I call 911; I think you are having a heart attack' just isn't necessary. Say: 'I am going to call 911; I think you are having a heart attack' and perhaps save your friend's life."

"Assertive language gives both the message sender and the message receiver the opportunity of knowing what is being asked and of meeting needs at any given moment. It does take practice."

The Science and Art of Asking Questions

Kelly knows it is her turn: "One of the most basic communication skills is the ability to ask good questions. People apologize a lot for their questions e.g. "I hope you don't mind me asking . . . I know this seems like a stupid question but . . . 'I strongly suggest that you avoid putting yourself down with needless apologies or discounting your desire to know. It is perfectly ok to ask any question; most people know when to ask and when not to ask. It is the form of their questions that need some work.

"There are many different types of questions. One is a close-ended question that has a specific focus, seeking a specific answer. It is good for focusing on an issue and getting clear information. It relates to what the person wants yet doesn't allow a wide variety of responses. Alternatively, an open-ended question picks a subject area and allows for many responses. When you first meet someone or are greeting an old friend, use an open-ended question, such as 'Hi Betty, how are things with you today?' If you ask, 'Isn't this a great day?' you are really stating your opinion and are not asking about the other person. Another frequent miss-statement is: 'don't you just hate this rain?' That is a forced choice, closed-ended false question that is really a statement. If you want to know what the other thinks of the rain, ask, 'What do you think about it raining today?'"

"When you are not sure whether to use an open-ended or a closed-ended question, ask your question open-ended. You can always ask a follow-up closed-ended question if it is needed."

"Skill in communicating starts by being a good and active listener. Listen to the other person, not to yourself. 'Betty, I bet you don't like this rain' is someone who is listening to him/herself.'"

An Answer from Silence

Dr. D. identifies another important possible communication snafu: "A frustrating experience is to ask someone a question and not get a direct answer Often the other person will suddenly change the subject, look away, or do something else to avoid a direct answer. Even the repeating of the question often gets the same pattern."

"Recognize that there is non-verbal communication occurring here; it isn't what you are expecting, as you requested a verbal response, but it is an answer. Most of the time any of the above would be interpreted as 'No' . . . Kelly and I will demonstrate."

*   *   *

Dr. D: "Kelly, let's eat in for lunch today and have Chinese? Ready to go?"

Kelly doesn't answer the question asked as she is thinking about what she wants to do next and doesn't like Chinese food: "I have some errands to run; I'll be back in about 30 minutes."

Dr. D., frustrated, yet he started the confusion by making a question statement: "Wait, where does that leave me? Do you want me to wait 30 minutes for you to return or go on without you?"

Kelly is now aware of his anger but is still only thinking of herself: "I told Nana I would meet her at the flower shop about now and I don't want to be late as our favorite florist goes to lunch right at noon. Bye. I'll be back for our afternoon meeting."

Dr. D. "Well Sugar, X-ray, Foxtrot (a very old amateur radio response). What's next?"

*　　*　　*

Dr. D. comes back to his non-role playing self and continues: "In our 'do it wrong demonstration' Kelly did answer by avoiding the question for some reason, a reason we don't know. Be aware of almost never judging another's motivation as the professionals get that right only about thirty-three percent of the time. Focus on behavior, first by describing it and then asking specifically, again and again, for what you want. Now, we will demonstrate a good way to communicate on the issue at hand . . . I start off by talking to myself."

*　　*　　*

"This sort of communication has gone on too long between us. She has left my office but not cell phone range so I will call her . . . Kelly, glad to catch you. I really want to know exactly whether you are going to eat lunch with me or not? Obviously your meeting with Nana was prearranged and very important. Tell me, 'yes' or 'no', will you eat lunch with me today?"

Kelly is direct and to the point. She does not use the word "can't" and uses "will/won't" instead saying:: "I am very focused on meeting Nana; the poor communication is 'my bad." No, I won't eat with you today but will tomorrow. Let's get a group up tomorrow and share a pizza."

Dr. D. now has head a direct answer even though it is not what he wanted to hear. However, having Kelly affirm that she will again eat with him in the future, he responds with a good feeling. "That sounds good to me; we will plan it when you get back. Now I know you won't be here today and I feel better . . . darn, she hung up on me. That is not like her; she was really focused elsewhere."

*　　*　　*

"Our next focus will be on a very common argument that occurs often in human communication. Enjoy the dialogue and decide when a similar one was part of your dialogue. Remember, many things are not what they seem to be as shown with the 'last word.' Read it and think deeply."

The Last Word:
Not What You Think Nor When!

All family members engage in conversation. There are many secrets about what and how things are said and it is time to share one of the secrets; that is about "The Last Word." A family drama often begins with a minor argument. People argue all the time. Often one person stays the course and keeps arguing, discussing, or collecting information, no matter what is not stated nor whether someone is winning or losing. It is quite common for one person to suddenly proclaim: "You're impossible. You always want the last word!" They then often get quiet, have emotional time, or quickly move away.

The real one in control is actually the person who complained! Who gets the last word depends on the listener, not the speaker. The person claiming the other person always gets the last word allows that to happen by stopping speaking. If they didn't become quiet, but said something else, they then temporarily would have the last word. For example, observe this sports argument:

> John Bearister: "My Sea Hawks will beat your team badly next Sunday."

> David Bearister: 'No way; not if our QB is healthy again!"

> John Bearister: "Even with healthy QB's for both teams, we will clean up!"

David Bearister: "No way, our defense is too good."

This usually goes on for a while and then one arguer gets frustrated and claims:

John Bearister: "I'm tired of listening to you; you like to argue too much. You always, get the last word. Well, I'm done. I am not saying one more

David Bearister says nothing as he is stunned. Who actually got the last word?

In this case it was actually John Bearister although he stated just the opposite. What if this happened; after John Barrister's frustration and false accusing statement, David Bearister simply said: "Your right."

Who got the last word then?

And if John Bearister responded: "I know I am right!!" Who got the last word then?

Another optional "Last Word" tactic is for John Bearister to give out a strong emotion such as "Darn it, I've had it!" Remember, it isn't the words with emotions but the tone of voice, loudness of voice, and accompanying body language that count. He has substituted a "Last Word" with a "Last Emotion" although claiming he has been had. A good counter by either person is not to feel or speak about the subject of debate but to say: "Wow, you are really angry." Then they have the last word. "Probably." "Maybe.".

Actually this can go on for a long time. Another way to end it is to decide together who gets the last word and then stick by that agreement. However, that is easy violated. By agreement, John Bearister gets the last word, makes a final statement, and David Bearister. says: "Good, It's over."

I hope you have caught on by now and know without my saying that got that last word? A better way is to agree for both to count together out loud to five at the same time and then both move away to other places. Families would be better off if all knew about "The Last Word" and could decide to play or not.

"One Shouldn't Should" ☺☺
Or is it "One Shouldn't Should Not?"

This is another very common, value driven communication issue. As we have stated many times, values are always with us. A frequently used statement has to do with "should" and "should nots," which are one of the most frequently utilized value statements.Should statements in any form (need to, must, ought,) are statements about values that state some desirable behavior related to a value e.g. "you shouldn't talk with your mouth full", "you should dress better when you leave the house," "you need to lose weight." These are generalizations about someone that may or may not be true as presented. When any of the above statements are made about you, you are "being should on"; that isn't any fun. Say the phrase "being should on" out loud several times to get the pun intended.

There are different ways of dealing with the same issues with less of a value emphasis and more of a factual approach. For example, "you need to lose weight" can better be stated something like this: "Your general health would improve if you lost ten pounds" or "I notice you are walking slower; would losing some weight literally take some pressure off of your legs and feet?"

Unfortunately when people give their concern in a passive manner, the person listening hears the secondary message of "I'm telling you what to do" and often feels negatively. That dismisses an important message, deflects from the concern that is intended and overall doesn't allow the relationship to grow to its full potential.

Health personnel know that weight loss is complicated. There are eating issues, exercise issues, health issues, and economic issues to consider. The statement: "You should lose weight" is about the values of the person saying it, not at all about the issues the heavy person faces in getting back to a healthy weight.

Attitude Adjustment

It can be a fun project to set a goal of stopping all usage of the words "need to, must, ought to and should" and their corresponding negatives. As days go by, monitor yourself several times a day as to how you are doing in finding alternatives to those words that are not as judgmental as they are. When you find yourself making a mistake, say "Opps, I just 'shoulded' on someone." You may have to say that word out loud several time to get the intended pun and to offer the right tonal inflection. Instead, say: "My Bad." After about a week, most people avoid those 'should' words.

*   *   *

Dr. D. and Kelly return and Dr. D. promptly interrupts the Author's narrative: "You have offered much, 'but' it is time to end this column."

Kelly: "Oh, no, don't 'but' our boss. He will know he has just been 'butted'! Let us get out of here. Summarize, as always, and go have coffee."

Dr. D.'s Famous Summary

"Let's go, 'but' first, a quick summary:" Dr. D. can't help grinning; the last 'but' goes un-noticed. "We have identified basic communication snafus and what to do to break the patterns. This book offers things to improve on all those areas as we journey through life. Remember, there is always much to learn."

Kelly: "I will drive; come ride with me, but then . . ."

© 2013 Dr. D.'s Domains

Chapter Five

A Misstating/Mishearing/Misinterpreting Tale: A Classic Family Communication Issue

In real life, you don't react to what someone did; you react only to what you think she did, and the gap between action and perception is bridged by the art of impression management.

If life itself is but what you deem it, then why not focus your efforts on persuading others to believe that you are a virtuous and trustworthy cooperator?"

Jonathan Haidt

Saying "No, No, No" to Your Neighbor

Unlike before, John Bearister kept his appointment with Dr. D. this week. He arrived on time and found Dr. D. waiting for him with two cups of hot coffee. "I see Kelly got here before both of us," John exclaimed while sitting down and taking his first sip. "Did I get that right or did you make this great cup of coffee? Either way, I really welcome it."

Much to his surprise, Kelly stuck her head into the office and said: "Hi John, glad you made it. Speaking of making it, of course I did! I consider it one of my skills, getting the right brand of coffee, measuring just the right amount out, and putting in a corresponding amount of water. What has been our secret until now is that Dr. D. makes the second batch late in the morning so that we have enough for lunch. I will leave you two alone and go finish up the book chapter we have been working on regarding communication and the classic misstating, mishearing, or misinterpreting that goes on."

"Kelly, we love you for much more than your coffee making." Dr. D. affectionately spoke to an empty doorway as she had already left. "What a woman. We are so lucky to have her on staff. She will have that chapter polished and back up here in about an hour, with minor input from me. Anyway, let's start with you. What's on your mind?"

John sipped and spoke. "We agreed to talk about the calls Judy and I have been getting and she will do that next time when she comes in my place. This first time I want to share a hurdle we are having with our next door neighbors. Following what Kelly said, I think it is a communication issue. Barry and Jean are our same ages and their kids are also grown up. We like to do things with them but lately they are often mad at us because of things Barry said we told them, except we never told them what they claim. Sometimes they just don't hear it right, especially when Barry isn't wearing his new hearing aids; most of the time it is a misinterpretation on their part.

"The latest example of their misinterpreting came this past weekend. We had been talking about going out to eat with them which they wanted to do. I told Barry on the phone: 'We can help with all that you do that really ends up being stressful for you. Since you have been late to most things, let's go to dinner an hour later than usual so that gives you more time to finish up your other tasks.' Hearing that, he hung up on me and wouldn't answer the telephone when I called back. Judy finally went over there to talk with Jean about when we were going to go, and Barry yelled at her: 'No one calls me a poor planner; I always plan ahead and do what I say I will do.' It took some explaining by Judy to Jean and then Jean talking to Barry for him to realize that we didn't mean what he interpreted our offer to be. What I was doing was recognizing his full plate and offering to change our plans slightly to aid them in getting it all in. What he seems to have interpreted was that we were saying he didn't plan nor manage things well, which is far from what we think. We were trying to help and look what it got us—bitched at!"

Dr. D. paused, and then responded to John. "That is a tough place to be; I hope you got things quieted down so you could spend the evening together. In any case, that is a common occurrence between two or more adults. It will likely happen with your own extended family. It is interesting that you brought this example to us because this is exactly about what we now are writing. That you did bring it here is called 'Serendipity' meaning a happy accident or a pleasant surprise; an accidental find of something wanted but not expected (http://en.wikipedia.org/wiki/Serendipity). I think this fits our conversation; I find it happens often to me. This also gives me a chance to do exactly what we want to do with our chats and that is to offer information that will help you help others without telling you exactly what to do. That works best and I think that is what you want."

John nodded in agreement. "What is the information you want me to have?"

Dr. D holds up a finger, wanting John to pause, and quickly dials a three digit number. "Kelly . . . oh good, that is what I was calling about. You are finished with that chapter on communication snafus that we have been working on . . . Great, that is so timely. It fits John and my conversation perfectly so I said I would share it with him. As you were coming down here with it, would you bring an extra copy for John? Thanks," he finished up and hung up the phone.

"I think this is what you are looking for. We put it in a context that most people our age can connect to, a famous comedy routine. I'll let you take this home and Judy and you can read it and decide what you can use with your neighbors. Then, if Judy is coming next time in your place, we can start by hearing what you both liked and used or what didn't fit that situation. Is that agreeable with you?"

John replied immediately. "Yes, and I will get to thank Kelly for the coffee."

After several minutes Kelly stuck her head in the door, handed two copies of a manuscript to Dr. D. and John, and immediately left, going somewhere in a hurry.

John was glad to get the copy but disappointed that he didn't get to thank Kelly. After a few ending pleasantries, one they both knew wouldn't happen this week—"Let's do breakfast or lunch"—John left and Dr. D. immediately began reading his copy. Here is what he read.

*   *   *

The History of the Great Communication Snafu

Way back when, or at least when most of our readers were beginning to read books, there was a world famous comedy team named Abbott and Costello. They perfected the routine of having a straight man (when that term was not related to one's sexual preference) introduce a subject or topic of conversation and then the comic (the responder) replied not from what was said but either from what he pretended to hear or what he misinterpreted. Vivian Vance and Lucille Ball were also exceedingly good at these routines. For a younger audience, so were the Smothers Brothers, Dick and Tommy Smothers. Where did they get their ideas? From everyday life and regular human communication. They just jazzed them up and made them very funny to those people who listened carefully. Technically, what made it funny was the over and over-ness of the conversation where neither person moved from their part or their lines; they just kept changing examples, much as people in an argument do today. This is old time comedy that is very much alive in human dramas today.

Many people will tell you that one of the most famous and funniest comedy routines of all time, even up to the 21st century, is the 'Who's on First?' routine by Bud Abbott and Lou Costello. As the words alone cannot do the routine justice, they are not given here even though they are in the public domain. To read the words, go to http://www.baseball-almanac.com/humor4.shtml. As you are a 21st century reader and viewer, you have the advantage of being able to actually watch this legendary duo deliver their version of a common human communication routine via 'YouTube' at http://www.youtube.com/watch?v=sShMA85pv8M

As the YouTube version, the best one, doesn't give any background information, here is some background information to add to your enjoyment.

> The skit was originally done on the radio live (each and every time) until the legendary duo later included it on The Naughty Nineties compilation. The general premise behind the exchange has Costello, a peanut vendor named Sebastion Dinwiddle, talking to Abbott who is Dexter Broadhurt, the manager of the mythical St. Louis Wolves. However, before Costello can get behind the plate, Abbott wants to make sure he knows everyone's name on the team. **(http://www.baseball-almanac.com/humor4.shtml)"**

Now that you are back from enjoying the routine, we will explain how this chapter actually got written. Nana and Dr. D. were vacationing at Hilton Head Island and planning on writing a column on classic human communication issues. Before they settled down to write in the afternoon, they went for a swim in the ocean and actually had an Abbott and Costello type of conversation., without knowing that is what they were doing. Here is part of that conversation with some recipes about human communication and creative problem solving.

* * *

Nana and Dr. D. are Deep in Ocean Water and Communication.

As it always is around Hilton Head Island, the beaches are long and flat, gently sinking into the depths of the ocean. The water is fairly warm year around, thanks to the Gulf Stream that goes right by the Island. One can find shells in the sand, often alive with their habitants. It is a family beach with little swells, some waves but none really good for surfing. Looking back at the beach from the water, one sees lines of beach umbrellas all grouped together close to entrances to the tree-lined shore, about 200 sandy yards from the water. It is that way all around the island as the founders knew not to let people build right on the water. The sky is a rich Carolina blue, in reference to its northern neighbors. Nana and Dr. D. spent many summers here with their family and now are back as a couple enjoying a mid-summer week of beaching and writing.

"I can't wait to get into the water today because it was so nice and comfortable yesterday . . ." Nana exclaims to her husband.

In the ocean up to her knees, Nana shivers with cold and excitement. "This is great . . . Brrr. It is colder than yesterday."

Dr. D asks: "What is colder, the air?"

Nana: "No, the water," she replies.

The husband becomes the scientist and states scientifically: "Couldn't be the water. The temperature of the water here on July 4th is 84 degrees and the average air temperature is 89 degrees."

The conversation becomes confusing; they are not on the same page.

* * *

"What is 89 degrees?"

"The air."

"Couldn't be; you must mean the water."

"No, I meant the air, but we are now more in the water than the air. I am now in up to my shoulders and now I am fine. You are the one that is cold."

"I didn't say I was cold, just that the water was cooler than yesterday."

"But it couldn't be cooler because the water temperature doesn't vary that much, especially in the summer and certainly not day by day.

"Well, it feels that way to me."

"What, the water?"

"Well, maybe it is the air that feels different? But I am in up to my armpits and I am mostly in the water so it couldn't be the air."

*   *   *

"Maybe it's all in your head."

"My head? It's not even in the water."

"I didn't say that your head was in the water, I said this is all in your head."

"My head's not cold, and I repeat, it isn't in the water."

"Maybe you do have something there. Maybe it is your body temperature that is cooler."

"But how can that be? Normal body temperature is 98.6 degrees. Besides, how can one person's body temperature be making the whole ocean cooler?"

*   *   *

A narrator interjection: "Remember, this is all spontaneous. There is not a script . . . perhaps one of them does remember Abbott and Costello arguing the same way? Couples who have been married for years do this all the time.

*   *   *

Men are problem solvers so instead of enjoying the banter with his wife, Dr. D. turns scientist again and tries to straighten it all out: "Well, you are confusing everything and everybody. Actually, a human's body temperature varies from the part of the body where the temperature is taken. For example, temperatures taken from inside the body are different from those outside the body. Which one were you referring to? You know, we take temperatures both ways."

Could Nana be leading him on? She has her hands on her hips now and is about to give him one of her famous looks. Nana: "Please explain this to me because right now I am feeling cool on my legs yet warm above the waist. What is going on?"

Her husband bites, hook, line and sinker. "If you take your temperature in your ear it is likely to be different than that taken in a lower body spot. That doesn't make your inside or your overall external temperature different as they are really compiled averages where the average is very consistent and easy to remember."

Nana just wants to relax and enjoy. "Actually, I don't really care as to what makes this happen. I like the warmer feeling and want to feel that all over. Let's do something to stay warm."

Dr. D continues to think and expound to his wife and the fish: "I agree, 'what' answers are something that can come later . . . perhaps it rained warm water somewhere else and that warm stream just reached you. The other thing we could do is to swim a bit rather than just standing here. That might have us move with the stream that is flowing and it also raises our body temperature in all areas, which in turn, means that we are actually warmer."

*   *   *

Nana and Dr. D swim a bit, actually seeing some fish go by them, which they try and catch unsuccessfully. They begin to think that they are dolphins but tire before they either act like a dolphin or see one. Dolphins do come in close to shore and swim with humans, but not today. They finally stop, now up to their waist one moment, and then up to their shoulders as waves crash over them. What fun and it brings back many memories of ocean play as youngsters. Nana finally breaks the silence. "Maybe it is the jellyfish that are making the difference."

"Jellyfish? I don't see any jellyfish."

"Actually, I don't either. But we were told by other beach goers as we approached the water's edge that jellyfish were here. I don't think that anyone would make that up."

Now Nana is curious. "Maybe you just misheard them."

"No, I heard what I heard. Maybe they just misspoke and thought that there were jellyfish here."

"Or, there is another possibility and that is someone misinterpreted what another swimmer said. You know that happens a lot."

*   *   *

"Yes, there is much misinterpretation based on what a person thought that they heard but wasn't really said. Then again, a person can also misspeak on their own or a person can misspeak based on another person's misinterpretation. Or . . ."

Attempting to get the mood back they had when they entered the water, Nana redirects the conversation. "Let's give this all up and just enjoy the wonderful water again or go in and enjoy the beach, although now that we have gotten warmer or adjusted or something . . . I could stay out here all morning . . . but our editors are expecting a column out of us. What are we supposed to be writing about today?"

*   *   *

On task, D. D. states: "I brought our new Dragon dictation software so we can just speak our column while we are here at the beach."

Nana: "I didn't ask how we were going to write our column, I asked what we were writing on."

Dr. D: "Oh, I guess I was thinking about one thing so thought that I heard you say something else. I am glad that got clarified. Why do you want to know what we are going to write about? You are the one who sets up the writing schedule."

Now upset, Nana asks the big four questions. "Why? What? Where? When?"

Dr. D: "Why what? Where with Who? When? What are you talking about?

*   *   *

Looking puzzled, they both walk ashore to their beach chairs. As neither believes in apologies for minor misunderstandings or events, there are no apologies. Nana breaks the silence. "Let's start this conversation over again. I was very confused and often when I get confused, I get mad. Being mad seems silly now but I know it happens with all of us," she says, still miffed.

Her husband knows that line has been crossed and works to clear it up. "Mad? At Whom? Me? Why? Anyway, none of this matters because if you are mad, that will cancel out any thinking. If feelings dominate, that always trumps logic."

*   *   *

Figuring Things Out

They are on vacation so we leave them there to enjoy and hopefully not miscommunicate too much. What they will end up writing on today is about the complexity of human communication and how mix-ups are quite common among family members or even couples. Family members and/or couples become so used to listening to each other that their listening skills are abandoned or not utilized. They listen actually to themselves instead of the other person(s). Couple and/or family communication can become quite complex, with feelings involved. Often blame starts with everyone blaming the other person(s) communicating. However, blame doesn't get anyone anywhere because after blame, you still have to commit to change what you don't like. Furthermore, since most people will change best when they feel good about themselves or positive about something, they seldom will change if they feel attacked.

We know that human communication is tough especially when single examples are thrown in to attempt to prove a point. Humans love their "single case examples," which hold water (pun intended) for that example but often don't translate over to other situations. Dr. D. and Nana know that there are three things that most often go wrong with communication: (1) The speaker can misspeak and say something wrong or inappropriate for the situation; (2) the listener can mishear what was said and actually think something else was said and/or (3) the listener can misinterpret what was stated and blame the speaker for erring when it was really the listener who made the mistake. Notice two out of the three mistakes belong to the listener. If any of these three possibilities exists, that then brings up a similar dilemma in that both parties are arguing, and think that they are right. Remember the old army saying, "Any order that can be misunderstood has been misunderstood."

Recipes for Change

Dr. D. and Nana have often worked to help people improve listening skills by having the listener state back to the person who just spoke what s(he) heard them say before offering your own thoughts or feelings. Professionals call this "reflecting." One can either state what you heard about a thought or a feeling. e. g., "I am hearing that you are upset with me" or adding information, "I am hearing that you are upset with me for not coming to your party." Once they agree that is what they heard, and it is what you stated, then you can go on to what you wanted to add. If again what they said they heard was not what was intended, then seek their willingness to listen to you all over again and repeat the above. If you can say the same thing, but in slightly different words, that is often better.

Another recipe focuses on creative issue-solving using well established recipes for this process. The process does not involve picking a winner, or pointing a finger, as most people want to, but changing the way each states views or positions. Just like above, you could each say what you said again, but with different words. The goal again is not to pick a winner, but to get consensus about each one of you has heard and comprehend the other's opinion. Then, when all agree on that summary, both can move forward one step and together decide what is the common ground. That in turn will lead to what to do about the topic at hand. Many people call that creative problem-solving. The process of doing creative issue-solving is quite standardized and one version even has been named: "Synergetics." http://synergeticscollaborative.org/or http://en.wikipedia.org/wiki/Creative_problem_solving"

It is Not the Technique But the Solution That is Creative.

Our emphasis has been on how hard it is to speak with clarity as well as listen accurately. It's almost a lost art. In addition, as has been stated before, modern communication devices, such as email and texting, often make communication muddled since these media's main strength is not clarity-enhancing but ease of initiating or responding to a message. The best use of email and texting is for one-way communication or past-timing. When a discussion is in order, talk in person or over a telephone. Today, talking via a cellphone can be done with much ease.

Our lead couple has walked ashore with a couple of sand dollars, but luckily no jellyfish as they are poison to the touch. Nana continues to attempt to get her husband to give up the work for a while . . . but even she ties work with pleasure: "To move us creatively forward, let's go have some fish for lunch since we are at Hilton Head Island. After lunch, before going back to work, we could go to the early show where that neat young magician is performing; perhaps he can help us think of ways of helping our readers do the creative work as magicians are always so straight forward in their approaches to their audience," she offers, with a cunning smile.

Dr. D: "Your buying?" Nana: "It's your turn." Dr. D: "I think you miscounted," he jokes.

"In closing, remember communication in a family can be very complicated. It is human nature to blame someone else when things are not as the other party wants them to be. In the end, doing something about issues that come up because of communication problems is what is important. That is the way things are with communications. We provided so recipes or steps one can take to change them. Remember, there is always more to learn."

©Dr. D.'s Domains 2013

Chapter Six

Becoming Assertive: Getting to 'Me' Without Stepping on 'Thee'

Weakness of attitude becomes weakness of character.

Learn from yesterday, live for today, hope for tomorrow. The important thing is not to stop questioning.

Dr. Albert Einstein

Seen, Heard, But Unknown

Dr. D. was busy filing away some papers when he heard a knock. He knew the door was open and the person he couldn't see must be John Bearister. But no one came in. There was someone there, but nothing was being said. "Hello . . . Hello, I say . . ." Thinking out loud: "That's strange. I am here. Whoever is out there should be 'hello-ing' me." Still nothing was heard.

Dr. D. went back to filing papers and then heard something drop in the hall. Now he had to go and see. He walked to his door and there was a young man, dressed in a suit and tie, bending over to pick up a book. "May I help you?" said Dr. D. The young man looked around, as if there were several people behind him, waiting to be called upon. That was not the case. "My name is Hubert Hummer, and I am here to see Dr. D. I have an appointment arranged by my Uncle John. I saw you working but didn't want to disturb you so I stepped back to figure out what to do."

In response, Dr. D. said: "I am Dr. D. This is the doorway to my office. I would be more comfortable inside. Come in." Hubert didn't move. "Is it OK to come in? You seem very busy."

"Well, technically, yes I am. I have a lot of projects underway, but actually, no. This is John Barrister's time and he isn't here."

Hubert spoke, unprompted. "He is here," he said flatly without any real emotion or energy to his voice. And then finally . . . "He is parking the car."

Dr. D. decided that words weren't going to move Hubert into his office. He stuck out his hand to shake hands but then he grabbed Hubert's hand and pulled him into the office, to the chair where he wanted Hubert to sit. The young man took the large hint and sat down.

Dr. D. went back to his seat and smiled to himself, remembering the time when another shy young man was invited to his office by a long wave of his arm and hand as if Dr. D. was directing traffic. That young man moved quickly and sat in the large leather chair that was clearly the doctor's. Dr. D. remembered how he got confused over that so he sat down in one of his visitor's chairs. He waited for the visitor in his chair to start the interview as that was the protocol of that chair . . . Dr. D. quickly brought himself back to the moment and was about to speak when Judy Bearister stuck her head in the door.

Another surprise. Dr. D. motioned her in and she knew where to sit, in one of the other comfortable chairs. "I didn't expect you. Hubert said that John was coming."

Judy didn't hesitate. "John is going, not coming. He is flying out in thirty minutes to speak at the writer's conference down at Vegas . . . you remember, don't you? John sent you two emails about this last week. Since we didn't hear back from you, we thought it was OK."

*   *   *

And Now the Rest of the Story[12]

If I write this all out as it happened, it will take the whole chapter just to find out who Hubert is, why John didn't bring him in and introduce him and why he is there. I'll report it much more quickly than would a verbatim transcript. Hubert Hummer is a twenty-two-year-old graduate with a two-year degree from our community college and a major in psychology. He can't find a job as a counselor, as would be the case of anyone with those minimal credentials, and certainly not anyone with his considerable passive personality attributes and traits. Dr. D. did not get any emails. John Bearister knew that Dr. D. didn't do counseling in their meetings. The sessions were more designed to talk about situations that were shared by family and friends. Information and recipes were his outputs now.

Eventually, Judy explained much more about Hubert's many passive behaviors and life experiences and that he had little idea how to mine some of his assets to find and hold a job. Dr. D. sent Hubert back to see his Community College counselor who knew him and with whom he had a relationship. He did give Hubert a draft copy of a list of books Kelly and he were compiling that dealt with assertiveness and communication. It was quite clear that regardless of what else was needed, Hubert Hummer had to learn some basic communication skills.

This time Hubert did shake Dr. D.'s hand and spoke his thanks. Judy and Hubert left to go back to the community college; Dr. went back to work, still not knowing what prompted John and Judy to bring Hubert rather than talking about his needs as the situation of the week. This is a typical example of a very passive man seeking to have his mind read.

---

12 Thank you Paul Harvey for days and days of great comment and reporting. http://en.wikipedia.org/wiki/Paul_Harvey

Ah, some of Kelly's great coffee just arrived via Squire Bin Forever of England, the newest member of the Forever Family team. To ground our focus, here is background information on the assertiveness communication recipe.

Learning the Assertive Communication Recipe

People relate to each other in a style and manner learned in their childhood, typically patterned after how their Mom and Dad went about maintaining and developing relationships. That pattern served them well up until their offspring became emerging adults or young adults with all of its changes and nuisances. Even though the new adults now hold the power position in relationships, they are likely to use the communication methods under which they were raised. Parents of emerging adults will often benefit from a style change to assist them in obtaining autonomy in their own lives. To help them learn a new method of communication, they will need a lot of information along with the experience of a mentor or someone who knows the recipe of assertiveness and knows how to help people learn.

The Aggressive Form and Style of Communication

It is possible that they were using an assertiveness communication recipe previously; however, it is more likely that the previous style of communication and relationship molding was either one of aggressive behavior or passive-aggressive behavior. Aggressive behavior comes about when one person is able and needs to "direct the show" by making most decisions in a relationship. It is what parents typically do when parenting young children because only they have the experience and mental capacities to make the complex life decisions. When a parent has young children, s(he) may seek their opinions but it is the parent who makes the final decision. That decision forces the actions and behaviors of the youngster to comply.

Being aggressive in an adult world is about dominance. It is about doing things one way, the aggressor's way e.g. John and Judy Bearister were invited to the home of some new friends for the evening. When they get there, after a few pleasantries, their host said: "We have this new game called Mexican Train. We would like to play it with you. Bring your drinks and come to the game table where we have the game setup." This aggressive invitation, an order, typically results in passive responses from the other couple, as they do not want to play this game or any game, but feel ordered to do so. They then complete their passive response by dutifully playing the game and, as soon as possible, find an excuse to leave. They carry out one last passive act of social conformity by saying: "We had a good time; thanks for inviting us."

On their way home, John and Judy complained to each other about being forced to play the game and offered the comment: "It will be a long time before we go back there and we certainly won't invite them over to our house." Being dominated in any situation was not something they liked (most people don't), but a passive response in this situation seemed better than being aggressive. Neither of the couples knew about being assertive so that was not an option.

The Passive-Aggressive Form and Style of Communication

Some persons favor using a combined passive-aggressive pattern of communication. Here, the form is passive in nature but the style is aggressive. Looking further, their style is active, with lots of energy but done in an adapting way. An example would be this statement by Dr. D: "I am so glad we get to see you tonight, what are we going to do?" Then, if asked for his/her opinion, the response is quickly made.

Judy: "I don't know, I haven't thought that far ahead. You decide." Through that brief exchange, the questioning and the response was passive. Although many men take a passive-aggressive approach, it is more often used by females.

An additional example will help explain this form and style. Judy's stepmom wants her to come over for the day but not until her favorite morning television show ends. She calls Judy and says: "I don't want to overly influence your plans for the day, but you are long overdue in coming over here. I arranged for lunch to be sent in; you will come of course—after 11:00 a.m." This is a fake apology and is a disguised act of aggression; questions many times are not question-questions but hidden statements."

Using statements that are known as socially acceptable statements e.g. saying excuse me while pushing one's way to the front of a line, and the famous "I'm sorry to interrupt" . . . hides the aggression being expressed by the person starting the demand. The demanding person is working to guide the recipient into doing what s (he) wants her/him to do without putting oneself at risk. This approach disrespects the other individual, not allowing for a relationship to form. There is a middle path between aggression and passivity that best respects and promotes moving to more in-depth relationships. That path is to behave in as assertive manner both in form and style. An assertive approach by Judy's stepmother would have been: "I miss your company and would like some today. I am busy until 11:00 a.m. Would you come to lunch today after 11:00 a.m.?"

Historical Assertive Communication & Leadership Models

Many classic examples of assertive behavior in history provide guidance and inspiration. Gandhi and Dr. Martin Luther King readily come to mind as both were leaders of oppressed, displaced groups who were dominated by an upper social class. In Gandhi, it was British colonials, and in Dr. King's situation, it was the American white establishment.

Both leaders came to the realization that submission to ruling powers was not working; something drastic had to happen. Both leaders chose a path of non-violent resistance—that is what makes their behavior assertive rather than aggressive and what separates them from run-of-the-mill freedom fighters. Both stuck to the posture of assertive protest despite becoming targets for escalating violence against themselves, their families, and the people they represented. In the end, both succeeded in making important reform occur, even if only imperfectly. Changes occurred through assertion. (http://www.mentalhelp.net/poc/view_doc. php?type=doc&id=9778)

Characteristics of Assertive People

Experts look at characteristics of assertive people. When one is behaving assertively:

- You feel free to express feelings, thoughts, and desires;

- You can initiate and maintain good relationships with a variety of other persons;

- You have control over anger. This does not mean that angry feelings are repressed; just the opposite, one controls anger by owning it, expressing it and discussing it with others in a calm and cool manner;

- "Assertive people . . . Are willing to compromise rather than wanting their own way and tend to have good self-esteem." (Marie Reid/Richard Hammersley, "Communicating Successfully in Groups (Psyc. Press, 2000, p.49);

- "Assertive people enter friendships from a 'Counting my needs and your needs' position."(Henry Virile, "Speaking the Truth with Love (2009), p. 48-49, 74).

Cultural Differences Influence Communication Styles

Having an awareness of the larger context or picture that surrounds any single event is something that distinguishes individuals who are assertive from those individuals who are not. Assertive people know that cultural differences greatly affect anything and everything. The communication norms and examples offered here are based on norms of a Western cultural setting. Interpersonal communication processes from this culture may conflict with values of persons from other cultures, including persons from other cultures living in this country. Thus, what one intends from an assertive approach, because of value differences, may result in the recipient interpreting your new assertive approach quite differently than what you intended.

Other cultures strongly value nonverbal communication as being the more important communication medium for them. Individuals from Latino, African/African American, Arab, South American or French backgrounds tend to stand much closer together when conversing than do European Americans. In terms of facial expressions, demonstrating congruence between your inner feelings and outward expressions is important. It is important to know that in some cultures e.g. Japanese and Chinese, restraint of strong emotions such as anger and sadness is considered to be a sign of wisdom and maturity. Tone of voice also can show considerable variation. Many Europeans may be considered soft-spoken compared to Arabs. For example, traditional Asian cultures value subtlety and indirectness in communication. More direct or confrontational styles may be viewed as disrespectful and lacking in finesse. Finally, behaviors used to show that one is listening also vary by culture. African Americans may not always look at their conversation partner, nod their head or say "uh huh" to indicate that they are listening. The "take-home" message is that what is considered appropriately assertive can vary by culture. Be thoughtful about how your own cultural background and those of others may play a role. (http://ccserver4.ad.uinc. edu/?page_id=187).

Specifics of an Assertive Form and Style of Communication

Listed below are eight different assertive communication and/or relationship building tools that have been used since this recipe was introduced in the 1960s:

Assertive Communication Method One

- **I-messages.** I-messages are the foundation for use with any of the other seven related tools. It is a direct, honest and factual way of communicating that has the best chance of being heard. An I-message is one where you begin your sentences with the word "I". You then either say what you are feeling and/or what you want. This approach keeps you from expressing a judgment about the other person or blames your feelings on them. Examples include: (1) "I am feeling _____" (Fill in the blank with a one-word feeling);

  (2) "I am feeling _____that you didn't return my phone call until at least 24 hours went by." The feelings felt are now supported by an action or behavior that went along with my feeling. These tools, the most basic of the eight, has you "own" your message by letting others know that it comes from you and that you aren't blaming them. There is a big difference between saying "You are wrong," than saying "I don't agree with you."

Option A: I-messages come in two forms. First, the most powerful, direct statement of your feelings would be: "I feel _____" (list the feeling). Do not attach any other information. Doing so will take away from the feeling being expressed. This feeling is yours and is not disputable, although others may well attempt to do so by saying something like this: "You shouldn't feel _____." Own your feeling and stick by it.

Option B: Make the same I-statement and link it to an event or behavior e.g. "I feel angry when you don't ever return my phone call." This is an assertive statement of feelings linked to an event or behavior. The message before the "when" states the feeling; the message after the "when" lists the event or behavior that corresponds with the feeling. "When" is used instead of other adverbs as it reduces the chance of blame being heard. Use this option when you want to discuss the behavior or event in question as that being last in the statement has the highest chance of being what the immediate next discussion will be about.

One other option is at the end of using these related tools, ask: "What did you hear me say?" If they don't know or stumble around, repeat your I-message and then repeat this question. If necessary, do the two-step routine several times.

Assertive Communication Method Two

• **Broken Record.** Often when you use one or more I-statements, the listener doesn't listen to you but listens to themselves. What that occurs, respond by saying: "You're not hearing me." If necessary, repeat several times like a broken record.

- This popular tool come from the 1960s when vinyl records used to stick on the record player and kept repeating themselves over and over. This is what you do; you keep repeating yourself when the other person in the relationship is being aggressive or passive. An example would be: "I am hearing how angry you are at me." If the other person hears you but continues to berate you, state: "I am hearing how angry you are at me." Repeat as often as needed until the other person shows a sign of hearing you, not just listening to them.

Assertive Communication Method Three

- **Ask for Feedback.** Start with an 'I-statement' and then say: "I want your view, your opinion. Tell me about how we can better communicate with each other." Here you are taking an emotionally-charged criticism or blaming from another and owning it via an I—message but then moving the conversation on by going back to them with the message "I am listening to you; let's problem solve, not just blame." You are encouraging them to be clear, direct and specific in their feedback to you.

Assertive Communication Method Four

- **Going Off on a Tangent.** This approach is one of misdirection and diversion. What you do is to pick one aspect of a criticism or an attack and speak to it. e.g. "Oh, yes, about the check to the Smith's that you think I miswrote, that was the fifth check I wrote that day. Every time I wrote a check, the checkbook cover broke and fixing that took a lot of time. Do you know how frustrating that is?" Use a lot of words, acknowledge that you heard what the other person said but work to get the focus on some other aspect of the criticism than your accuser wants. This is also related to "changing the paradigm" or basic belief system behind specific points, an approach of debate and thoughtful arguing.

Assertive Communication Method Five

- **Fogging.** This approach is one of distraction where you pick a criticism made towards you and say that you agree with that point. An example is: Criticizer: "If you had paid more attention to the dates you wrote the check and to whom it went, it wouldn't have gone to the wrong address. There you go, being dumb again and getting it all wrong!" Responder: "Oh, I did talk to your partner on the writing of the checks, and he gave me a different date. I was confused and I did error there. 'My Bad.'" Repeat several times if necessary. If the criticism continues, go to the next related tool.

Assertive Communication Method Six

- **Negative inquiry.** This is another diversionary tool. Start with: "Tell me more. How am I always messing up the checkbook? It is important to me that I get it right." Your goal is to defuse the criticism by asking for more of it. This seems to be just the opposite of what you should be asking. You are again dealing with the process by asking the person to think, to get into their cognitive domain, by confusing them by not reacting with emotion to their emotion as they actually want, and by focusing on something specific in their message to you.

Assertive Communication Method Seven

- **You're Right.** This brief, very effective assertive tool has you simply and quickly agreeing with a criticism without getting defensive or emotional in return. "You are right; I messed up those checks." Once you state that, be prepared for the other person to repeat his/her attack or expression of their feelings. This response is best given several times; "You are right; I messed up those checks."; "You are right; I messed up those checks." Once the criticism stops, follow with a response that changes the subject or that actually leads to a non-emotional, non-dominating "You are right; I screwed up those checks." I am working to slow down when I write checks. Any ideas on how to do this?" This follow-up response is asking for advice, which others love to give.

Assertive Communication Method Eight

- **Negative Assertion.** Begin this approach saying "You are right" then switch to what you want to talk about or approach; your need. e.g. "You're right. I have problems writing checks. I'll see what I can do about that. I do need more money put in the checking account every month. How can we get that done? We talk about doing that but never seem to get it done." The ending focus is on what you want, not about the complaint.

*　*　*

Final Adoptive Steps of an Assertive Form & Style of Communication

Kelly greets all: "Welcome back everyone. Opps, to be technically correct according to today's recipe, I would have said; 'I welcome you all back' as assertive people use 'I' statements."

Dr. D. "No, you are just fine. As with anything, there is a time and a place to use each recipe and the related tools. What I recommend for everyone is that you pick a recipe and use it often enough to the point that you know it well and can use it correctly. Then, add a second recipe to your repertoire and so on. The assertiveness recipe is a good starting point.

Kelly smiles as Dr. D. has told her about Hubert and this morning's meeting. She knows what she is going to say fits Hubert. "Making the switch to an assertive style of communication and relationship building is complex. I recommend that you take these steps when you are ready to make a change:

(1) Practice using the tools in a low stress situation instead of using them for the first time in a real situation. Find a friend or partner who knows what you are practicing and will communicate in an aggressive manner and let you respond assertively. Process what you experienced, what you did, what you did well, and where you had your difficulty. Focus on what you did well more than focusing on any difficulties. Always seek to increase one of your strengths. Repeat the process of practice several times until you get automatically good at it."

(2) Read one or more of these books on the topic. They are all well-known and have good reputations. Don't worry if the book is more than ten years old; little has changed in this process since it was started way back in the 1960s. (en.wikipedia/wiki/ Assertiveness)"

Alberti, Robert & Emmons, Michael L. (2008) You're *Perfect Right: Assertiveness and Equality in Your Life and Relationships (9th edition).* California: Impact Publications.

Bishop, S. (2006). *Develop Your Assertiveness (2nd Ed.).* Philadelphia: Kogan Page Publishers.

McClure, J.S. (2003). *Communication with Backbone . . . Not Bite.* Denver: Albion Street Press.

Paterson, Randy J. (2000). *The Assertiveness Workbook: How to Express Your Ideas and Stand Up for Yourself at Work and in Relationships.* Oakland, California: New Harbinger Publications.

Townend, A. (2007). *Assertiveness and Diversity.* New York: Palgrave Macmillan.

Virkler, H. (2009). *Speaking the Truth with Love: A Christian Approach to Assertiveness.* Xulow Press (www.xulow.com).

Dr. D.'s Famous Summary

Dr. D.: "Communicating assertively in form and style gives you the best chance of being heard by most people. However, there are some people you just have to walk away from. Using these recipes, plus others found elsewhere in this book, will help your life be the best it can be. That is the way things are with assertive behaviors and other not so good communication approaches. I have offered explanations of the way things are and what to do. It is good that you are learning now in your life as there is always more to learn. Goodbye."

Kelly likes his summaries, but today she wants the last word: "Goodbye, you all."

© Dr. D.'s Domains 2013

Chapter Seven

The First and Last Word Issue:
Which One Do You Want?

*When my monologue is long, those who are listening
are often confused, get lost, or get left behind.*

Dr. Dennis Cogswell

Sharing Emotions is Great Fun

Hot Damn! And *it's Show Time.* These are two things I say when I am excited. Lately, I have added *Families are Forever*, as writing our books is central to my life. Do the three go together? Absolutely. It's a fast-paced world today. Families cram an awful lot into a day. Do we complain about it? Of course. Do we keep on trying to do it all? Yes. Do I understand how come it is this way? Somewhat but this is not the time to detail those reasons.

Hot Damn! *It's Show Time* and *Families are Forever* have much in common. As words of feelings, they are words of excitement or they are exciting places to be. They also are short words and phrases that are attractive to Americans in our sound-bite world. I experience them as terms of endearment, love, and belonging. Some of the exciting times in my lifetime include:

> When I got married. The words—*I Do* and later, when my wife, Nancy, and I were alone, *We're Married*—are still vivid in my mind.

> When my first daughter arrived. That phone call when I heard: *You have a baby girl!* It meant I was a Dad; my own family had really started. I had a daughter to love. Oh, my.

When my second daughter arrived. I heard: First, *it's a girl*. Then Nancy and I simultaneously said as she held our fifteen-second old daughter. *We did it!* Euphoria.

When my son arrived. I was also right there to hear the words every Father-to-be longs to hear: *You have a son. I can enjoy being a father to both daughters and sons* I thought.

Hot Damn, It's Show Time and *Families are Forever* have an element of time to them. The first is a "now" term. It indicates that I am very much into "now", the moment, what I am doing right then. The second term has the word "time" in it and is both a word of "now" and a word to the future. It means something important is beginning. I first started using that when I was the coach of my son's soccer team and continued it as the head referee when I started a soccer match. The players loved the excitement it portrayed.

The third phrase has an element of time to it, an element that is hard to comprehend. Does "forever" really mean forever as in infinity? How can something last always? Doesn't it have to have a beginning and an end, as our dualistic thinkers, old school, want us to believe? When one begins to look at "time", one soon finds oneself looking at philosophical issues and approaches that philosophers think can lead us to a world of a higher level of consciousness.

The three phrases are also terms of connectedness as there is more than one person involved. Yes, I am the only one who says *"Hot Damn!"* but my frame of reference is one that involves other people. Other people lead us to communication and relationships, two of the themes of *Families are Forever.* Certainly, you picked up on the intense emotion.

There is much more. However, I am only going to deal with one more aspect before Dr. D., Nana, and Kelly take over. That element again is "time", only examined in a different way. We use time to structure our lives. It has been well-researched that order is important to humans, and very important to families. All humans have a need to structure their present time usage and to plan their future time usage. When we celebrate a birthday, we are celebrating many things: a person, an event, an accomplishment, a completion of an important segment of time. When a family loses a parent due to death or to divorce/separation, the members are not only losing a person, they also are losing structure and a way of doing things.

We talk a lot about relationships throughout the series. However, one can't separate relationships from communication nor from feelings, our other two themes. Relationships are also about structure. In this chapter we deal with some different aspects of structure than elsewhere. We are calling them (1) the last word, (2) the first word, and (3) the unexpected word. I hope you enjoy what you experience and learn. Thank you for being a part of our time, our structure, our relationship, as we communicate with you via the written word. You are so important. Always remember that, here and in the other parts of your life.

Reveille

Reveille is the name of a bugle call made famous in our armed forces that occurred every morning to awake the troops to their next day of activity. When that occurred, it was hated for what it brought and loved for its beautiful sound. Reveille signaled a change in time from night to morning, from sleeping to getting ready to be a military man/woman.

Some have suggested it could be played every morning on college campuses as their day starts. It might help with a serious problem. Getting life started. Scheduling. Making the most of one's twenty-four hours. For many students, this is a new responsibility. Most will have classes scheduled anywhere from 8 a.m. to evening classes that may last until 10 p.m. Students like the late morning classes as that lets them sleep late. Char, our sophomore student, and his parents started a pattern way back in high school that is not unique to them. As a high school sophomore, five years ago, he stayed in bed asleep every morning until his mother, Jolene, called to wake him up for his first class. Char was quite a night owl and partied a lot at night. The few evenings that he did study, he never seemed to get it together until after 11 p.m., a time when many were going to bed. His Mom was a great Mom in his eyes, and didn't say much to him about his bad habits as long as he got a minimum of "C's", which he usually did. Several times he had tried dual alarm clocks but didn't seem to get them set for the same time. Jolene knew that she shouldn't be doing this but was worried that he would flunk out if she didn't. She hoped he would mature sometime.

*   *   *

This was the story John Bearley, Dr. D's next door neighbor, told within five minutes of their sitting down with the good doctor for their weekly discussion. That appointment came about because John and Judy are the spokespersons for a Colorado chapter of Empty Nesters that Kelly, his colleague, and Dr. D. spoke to in Chapter One. They liked Kelly, Nana and Dr. D. so much that they asked them to answer questions about common family issues their group members were having. The three family specialists agreed. When word got out in their home community that John and Judy were bringing questions to them and information back, help was requested by dozens of parents not at the empty nest stage. It was beginning to become overwhelming to the Barristers.

"What do you think, Doc?" John asked, sipping the good coffee that they always had at the Families Are Forever Complex. "Jolene is a friend of Judy's and she called us with this issue late last week after someone called her a 'helicopter Mom' at a church luncheon. Jolene didn't know what this meant so she web-searched it. The term refers to a parent who hovers over their adult children and does too many things for them, making her a helicopter parent, one who means well but turns out adult children who are losers . . . Is this really a term people use? Could this story actually be true?"

Dr. D. paused and rolled his eyes upward. "Yes, Mom and son are too dependent on each other and she is doing things few mothers will do for an adult son . . . I suppose you are looking for me to give you a solution to the sleeping son situation? I could give a quick one, but this is very complex and likely not the only place where Mom is over supporting her son. It would be my estimate that she has been a helicopter mom for some time, and in many ways. It may seem like that is her problem alone, but we know nothing about the father as a parent. The son is an adult with responsibilities for his own education and his life style. Without that information, little should be done until a complete assessment is completed. I would help Mom realize that she and her husband need to see a family counselor while Char goes to his Student Counseling Center."

John nodded in agreement, shook hands with Dr. D, and left, happy again for the help.

Kelly came in immediately after John left, with her coffee and sat down. "That is one of the more serious cases of dependency I've heard but by no means an unusual situation for families. There is a thin line one walks between being a parent in a helping, loving, teaching, giving way and being an enabler.[13] It is something that I am constantly helping families and they all say: 'I see ___[X] is needed. What should my role be in making it happen?'"

---

[13]   This term can have both positive and negative meanings. For families, we use it as a negative definition which is to describe someone or a behavior that means well yet ends up creating unnecessary dependency.

Dr. D. had been thinking the same thing. "I think we could look at many elements here, feelings that help or hurt us, relationships that are great or too intense, and communication that is offered clearly but not received clearly. For me today, I will focus on the last one, communication."

* * *

The Last Word: A Great Ending

All family members engage in conversation. There are many aspects to conversation about what and how things are said. One of those aspects is about "The Last Word." When that becomes an issue, we say we have a drama underway. Often that drama begins with a minor argument. Arguments are often about control and feeling important rather than about the argument topic.

A story Dr. D. loves to tell is as follows: Once, a client, a father of three grown children, came to see Dr. D. because he had an ongoing argument with each of his three grown kids that never got resolved. He always withdrew from the arguments, in essence "placating" his offspring. This got him temporary relief but also long-term pain as the arguments were repeated and repeated.

He really wanted the last word when finalizing his will. Known only to his lawyer, he prepared a CD with his main points addressed to each of his offspring. He got very angry on the CD at his offspring and his wife at times. His instructions to his lawyer were to show the CD at the reading of his will and then read the will.

Luckily, his lawyer previewed the CD and telephoned the surviving wife. As the CD had no bearing on his will's dispositions, they decide that it could not do the family or him any good. It was announced at the will reading that he had left a CD-based video, but a deep scratch prevented it from being played. Then the wife/ mother stood up and said that she would share with them all one thing that their father liked and admired about each. She did just that. The will was read and the legality of the matters was upheld. All left the meeting talking about how good they felt about a deceased father who recognized strengths and shared them with all. Who did get the last word here?

Choices Abound and Must be Situational and Developmental Appropriate

Is this good or bad to have choices in relating to your adult offspring? Most experts say that the answer is situational, as it is with a four year old and her parents. Parents of young children know about this when they use the "red pants-blue pants" routine with their four year old who wants to wear a dress on a cold winter day. Time to leave for daycare is quickly approaching and Mom doesn't take the time for a teaching moment but simply wants to protect her daughter and get her off to school. The thoughtful mother says something like this: "Suzanne, it's too cold to wear a dress today. However, you may choose the color pants you want to wear. Would you like to wear the red or the blue pants?" If Suzanne does choose, Mom wins without Suzanne knowing that she hasn't exerted her independence. Mom better not overuse this as Suzanne will catch on and reply. "Ok, Mommy, I like red best, but I still want my red dress." Who is in charge now?

Our assessment today is that our society has repeatedly given our pre-eighteen-year-old offspring too much control over many aspects of their lives. They then rebel when parents set down rules related to driving a car, teaching life skills or managing normal life crisis. Examples of the latter include use of alcohol anywhere, especially while driving, the side effects of drug use, how premarital sex has become a recreational support with serious side e.g. communicable diseases, and the issue that the media is championing today and that is not texting while driving.

Parents don't have control as they did with younger offspring as the ability to be independently away from the parent changes everything. When our children were little, we got the behavior that we wanted through control. Starting with adolescence, to get the behavior we sought, we had to mix influence with control. However, rules can still be engaged and utilized, this time on the basis of discussion and contracting. Today's outcomes are not as important as tomorrow's. This is what Jolene didn't comprehend in our opening real life family situation. She was worried that her son would flunk out of college so she rescued him, time and time again.

Adult children, living on their own, often want to buy their own house, and often one that is way beyond their present means. They seek financial help from parents who give it with no contract about repayment or issue resolution. Again, these parents become well-meaning enablers.

Is saying "no" to our offspring of any age, wrong? Saying "No" often is claimed to be controlling, yet without it, bad things happen. There is a time at any age where wanting "to do it my way" has serious consequences.

Choice at any level doesn't automatically lead to learning. Neither does a lot of information. Albert Einstein said it correctly: "Information without experience is worthless." For example, your adult child wants you to loan them money so that they and their unmarried partner can buy a house together. You are pressured to do so. Our counsel would be only to consider this after all meet with a financial planner to gauge the consequences for all parties. Issues likely will arise. For example, what happens if this living-together-couple breaks up? Both persons in the broken relationship typically want to move on to new living arrangements so that they can put the past behind them. However, who owns the house? Who is going to make those house payments in a market where it may take years to sell a home?

In adulthood, games of competition become important for many people. Those who are serious game players of chess, bridge, baseball, and wrestling know that the first move influences all that happens afterwards. Good card players count cards and can know from one's first lead, what one is likely to hold that remains in your hand. Those persons who teach "Forensics" to high school and college students as they learn how to debate know that if two people are equally prepared and knowledgeable, the paradigm (an underlying belief) one argues from will be the key in who win the argument, or at worst, not lose it. Here is an example in the classic abortion debate.

> Ricardo: "I think it is clear that a baby is formed the moment a sperm fertilizes an egg. What do you think?"

> Joanne: "I think you are referring to a fetus, aren't you? Before we get to that, let's talk about who is going to make a decision about viability of a fetus. Will it be the woman, the mother-to-be, along with her physician, or the government? By the way, the last time you talked, you were very angry about government intervention so I am sure you won't advocate that here."

Already the serious arguing has begun, in a very classical manner. If Joanne responds directly to Ricardo's opening statement, she already is well along the path of losing the argument. However, she has been in this position before and has had good mentors. Fencing is a good metaphor for arguing. In this example, Ricardo thrusts and Joanne counter-thrusts. Her double-thrusts by setting him up for being anti-government. This will go on for a long time if these two continue to be as skillful as they have been in the first exchange. In all arguments, as is true for all of life, positioning is important. In family arguments, an underlying belief, called a paradigm, is what guides your points. If both arguers are equally informed on their positions, then what matters most is the belief system (paradigm) that wins.

Joanne knows this and works for her paradigm when she changes Ricardo's word "baby" to "fetus." She then continues by working to move the argument from Ricardo's "right to life argument" to her paradigm's "right to choose, right to control my own woman's body" focus. She works to set up Ricardo by telling him that she knows he is "anti-government" so he couldn't possibly want government involvement here. [14]

Contracting To Listen.

Who is in charge is a major issue in all adult-adult relationships. What we suggest is that when it is important not to let the natural leader speak first, to then "contract to talk". With this agreement, a debate changes to a discussion. Here is an example.

John and Judy Bearley have had a busy day at work. John is excited his colleague has offered to rent them his condo on their favorite Utah Lake for a very low price this summer. Judy has been told she will likely be promoted very soon. She wants to share that with her husband. Thus, both start to talk at once and in their excitement talk "at each other" for over ten seconds. Judy recognizes this first and puts her index finger up to John and says:

"John, we both are excited and we are not listening to each other. I have something very important to share and it seems you do also. Who should go first?"

---

[14] The Forever Family has a clear position on this classic controversy. Neither side is right or wrong. We advocate "continuous thinking" to help move us forward.

"Judy, you are right as usual. I am so tired of winter that I am thinking of summer vacation and boy did we get a gold mine tossed to us today, Michael . . ." Judy puts her index finger up and says, "John, it is obvious that you want to go first and I can wait a couple of minutes. Will you agree to briefly share what you have for a minute or two and then listen to me share for the same length of time?"

John says: "Sure, you will love what I am about to tell you and I will indeed listen to your good news. May I start again?" Judy puts down her index finger, nods yes, and turns her head slightly to let John know that she is now listening. She is assertive enough to again stop him and to share her news if he goes on and on. John has learned this about his wife and he loves her assertiveness, here and elsewhere! It will work out.

No Matter What, There is Always More To Learn.

It is important that people listen carefully to what is being said and not jump to conclusions. Much communication is complex and not what it seems. The word spoken is often NOT the word heard. What seems to be cause and effect may only be coincidence. What often appears to be one thing may really not be that way. Or what may appear one way to you may appear quite differently to another. Thus, don't judge. Evaluate. Ask questions. Listen well. Enjoy other people. Most often there is a story they will tell. Life is a story of stories. Just ask someone.

Dr. D.'s Famous Summary

Dr. D. always seems to know when to show up for the important final summary but he is nowhere in sight. I think we will have to share it ourselves today

A Reader: "We have focused on communication and told many stories. The timing of who does what is as important as listening. I hope you can use this information to make your life a communicative success. Remember, there is always more to learn."

Author: "Excellent job, reader. You stated it well. Dr. D. better look out or he may lose his job."

Chapter Eight

Tick Tock. The Clock Rules

*The only purpose for time is so that
everything doesn't happen at once.*

Time is an Illusion.

Dr. Albert Einstein

'Hickory, dickory, dock.
The mouse ran up the clock.
The clock struck one.
The mouse ran down.
Hickory, dickory, dock.'
By an unknown poet

Hickory Dickory Dock

This poem likely originated in the United States in 1774. It has never been used other than for what it was designed; a way to teach young children about the concept of time. If your offspring are having children of their own, you can recommend this poem as it has no known psychological reasoning or other agenda behind it; it is what it is. What seems attractive to young children, perhaps your grandchildren, is the repetition of sound in the first and fifth lines. It is not so attractive to adults who prefer a more complex repetition of sound such as is found in the adult's favorite: "A peck of pickled peppers . . ."

The Clock Rules

Westerners all live under the rules of a twenty-four hour clock. There are four main rules and they are absolute. All of us have tried to change each of the rules but been unsuccessful, as we knew we would be. They are:

Time Rule No. One: All people have twenty-fours in each day. Total. Period. This is a great equalizer as it applies to all persons, no matter our gender, race, religion, sexual orientation, financial status, or education level. We know this and yet have attempted to do something about it, whether the day is great or horrible. "Oh, what a wonderful time I had today; I wish it would never end!" "Oh, how boring today is; Please hurry up and end so I can go on holiday." This rule is ignored by people who try and do too much or who complain about all that other's do.

Time Rule No. Two: Twenty-four hours will go by no matter what you will do or will not do. A lot of people do not comprehend this. They have goals they want to accomplish and yet they spend their time wishing or list making rather than achieving what they want. The definition of a procrastinator is someone who is always late or who never finishes things. Achieving is very important to humans yet people don't use time well enough to achieve what they want.

Time Rule No. Three: The Past is gone and will not come back. The Future is yet to come but it will. Now is here, focus on it! So many parents, when they are with their grown kids, are in their physical presence but their minds are away back at work. They are thinking: "If I had only gotten that inventory report done . . ." or "If I had only gotten those reports typed, I would be in better shape for Monday." With this, the person moves back and forth between the past and the future but is not in the middle time, the present time or Now. They miss out on what is going on right at the moment. Some don't even care. They would rather re-feel the past or plan for the future than experience what they have or those with whom they're spending time.

Professionals who work with older family members that are experiencing severe memory loss really understand rule number Three. They bend it to help their patients with lots of present memory loss increase their ability to remember by helping them remember past items, even long, long ago times and to experience them as if they were back then. The last step is to get them to transfer their remembrance to the present time e.g. a ninety-year-old man is helped to describe the car he owned in 1925 and then to do the same thing with his most recent car. This is done so that once they dig deep in their past and to re-experience the past in some active way, they can be more aware or with it when they are at Now, in today's world.

Being in the past can be a positive event, and at the same time, a real detriment. For example, adult children and grandchildren will love it when you tell them stories, especially if you do it with humor. For a role model, listen to one of Garrison Keller's **A Radio Home Companion** radio shows, on Saturday evening around suppertime. People love good story tellers and now is your time to become one for your extended family.

The negative side of this is telling too many stories at one time. Your audience may soon get bored, resent you and tune out long before they will say anything. Telling stories from the past interferes with being in the *Now* and attending to what is going on right at that moment. Being in the *Now* is where you want to spend your time with your adult child and your grandchildren.

Time Rule No. 4: Everyone, in every moment of time, has to be somewhere. Somewhere may be either a real place such as in church or Fun Park e.g. Walt Disney World or an imaginary, virtual place e.g. Harry Potter's world. Rather than be in a real "somewhere", people are often lost in a memory, giving a "high five", observing who is in the same room with them, inside their head listening to their voices from their past order them to follow some rule, or fantasying about the future. How many times have you been caught "daydreaming" or been in a group where it was so obvious that someone else was doing just that? Doing that in the company of others hurts relationships as your companion(s) feel left out.

These rules get passed on from generation to generation through the way we structure our time when with our offspring. We pass it on when we raise our children to be the same way that we were, even though it may seem in adverted to us. With all that teaching, it would be very difficult for our adult children to change their patterns. If you want to influence their finding new ways of dealing with their time, instead of directly talking about this subject, take the approach that it is now time for them to add something to their life. Follow the truism: "When the student is ready, the teacher will appear". Be that teacher. Set your goal to help an adult offspring to be more aware, more spiritual, and more contemplative and model or demonstrate a "learning recipe" that you yourself follow.

Mentoring is a process of teaching by example followed by discussion of what the learner just experienced. We all are students in life. Learning, growth and development are lifelong processes. When mentoring, pick something basic and tangible such as working on the car of your son or daughter in a way not done before. Take the lead but don't do it all; your offspring need to do the majority of the work Avoid the role of a supervisor. Be a leader, teacher, and discussion leader. How you go about this is as important as what you do.

*   *   *

The Family Time Cycle

Our key characters and even our guest bakers have many thoughts about time, so let's see what they have to say, starting with Dr. D, Nana and then Kelly.

Dr. D: smiles as he knows that his behavior sends the real message. "I know that I was late getting here today and I found myself greeted accordingly. The first person I met said: 'Oh Hi, Dr. D., I am glad that you finally got here . . .' now I can take that several ways, just like our title: 'The Clock Rules' is a double entry. The greeting I received might be simply an acknowledgement that I had arrived or it could have been a 'soft' complaint that I was late.

"This book is about families viewed from the perspective of the 'clock rules/time'[15] issues we experience in the family of origin in which we grew up for around eighteen years of clock time. Ask any parent on how fast that time goes. During clock years zero to eighteen, we are primarily living with parents and siblings. When we become a member of our extended family, for eighteen to seventy + clock years, we have much more clock time.

"The older one gets, the faster clock time seems to go. For most people growing up is either a process of achieving certain milestones such as getting married or getting our first job or it is a result of age, most importantly ages eighteen, twenty-one, then twenty-nine, forty and finally sixty-five. Time is very important to us."

---

[15]   There actually are many kinds of time beyond clock time. Another one is developmental time, which is measured by human growth and developmental timelines being met. New mothers and their doctors are really interested in this. Our clock time and our developmental time may correspond or not. How many teenagers were ready developmentally to drive a car when fourteen? The hard one is the male adolescent who isn't ready to drive a car emotionally even at his clock age of sixteen.

Nana come to the front of the room and states: "It is my time . . . I am going to get us started so we use our time wisely by talking about raising your kids and/or your grandchildren. You likely have scheduled them to be very busy as youngsters and then as teenagers. We fill our children's/grandchildren's days with events such as soccer, dance, art classes, church groups, and so on. We teach them to be busy almost every waking moment. When you were sending them off to learn all these ways of doing neat things such as sports and dance, which were fun, you were adding to their time burden, then and now. What would keep them from not raising their offspring the same way when their kids come along? If they are not going to have children, then they will be very busy with other people. If you are being left out of their lives, then that is a result of conditioning, not that you or your offspring, has made a mistake. It is simply a matter of passing along the pattern. Everyone in our Extended families realizes that they are pretty heavy factors to have to face. No wonder adults of all ages often feel overwhelmed."

Kelly: "We know that with all there is to do in your life, you are going to feel and state: 'I'm Too Busy.' We will help with this issue that started several generations ago and those we all have inadvertently agreed to, yet from which we want out. Let's engage Dr. D.in banter to show this."

* * *

Almost a Con

Kelly: "Good morning colleague-of-mine; I missed you. You didn't show up for our work session yesterday."

Dr. D: "Well, I was busy."

Kelly: "Actually that was the second session in a row you missed. That really isn't like you."

Dr. D: "I was busy then, too."

Kelly: "I thought you might have called to let me know that you couldn't make it."

Dr. D: "I thought about it but when I went to call, something else came up . . . Oh, I know, I got a phone call I had to take."

Kelly uses her summarizing skills: "So a lot of things have gotten in your way and you didn't feel that you could communicate with me about what you were facing?"

Dr. D: "Well, I told you, I have been busy, with work, taking care of the kids and mowing the lawn . . . it just piles up every day. I just can't get anything done."

Kelly: "I think you are just 'playing' with me. This isn't like you."

Dr. D: "You got me, Kelly. It was hard to say with conviction what I don't entirely believe. However, this is a two-sided coin. Many people live in a jammed-packed world with never a free moment. There is also great misuse of the statement, 'I can't because I am too busy.' It is often used as a moral justification of not doing something. Let's look at both sides of that coin."

No 'Shoulds'

Kelly: "This ought to be interesting because I sometimes feel overwhelmed with life and it seems like I never get anywhere with what I have to do. It is a very bad feeling. Are you going to tell me that I shouldn't feel like that?"

Dr. D: "Kelly, that won't work. First, that would be 'shoulding' on you. I never do that. Your feelings are quite real and typical. Their feelings are real; what may not be real is what they think is causing those feelings. The events in their lives are a contributing factor, not a causing factor."

"I'm off to my next appointment and I know you have something to do, so let's let our Author surprise our readers with what we have figured out. It will include features of the way we lead our lives, what that does to us, offer some alternatives, and some adjustments to make. It won't be to cut back on activities or anything similar to that, but it will be related to changing a couple of things and adding or revisiting some previously known perspectives. You are up, Author."

*   *   *

Time is Relative to the Situation

Albert Einstein proved in the early 20th century that time was relative, not absolute. What did he mean by "relative?" Relative means everything being considered is evaluated by other variables, not on its own basis. He proved by scientific experiments that all motion is relative to the amount of time being measured. Time could differ for different people depending on the conditions around the measurement. The measurement was able to be more exact because atomic clocks were used. The laws of physics no longer followed dualistic thinking e.g. A OR B thinking but now used continuous thinking, A TO B thinking. That meant that single laws about space and/or time now had to be viewed from the multi-dimensional perspective—curved space-time. Time was influenced by the speed of what was being studied. He found that the actual time changed according to different speeds of contraction of that matter. Immanuel Kant holds that space and time "do not exist in and of them, but . . . are the product of the way we represent things, because we can know objects only as they appear to us." (http://en.wikipedia.org/wiki/Time) What does that have to do with being busy? The bottom line is that things time-wise are not as we believe them to be.

Parkinson's Law

Parkinson's Law has been around since 1955, yet many are not aware of it. It states "work expands so as to fill the time available for its completion." There are many off-shoots from it including the one that says, "Work will always expand to fill the time available for it." To read more about this, go to http://en.wikipedia.org/wiki/Parkinson's_law.

Assertive Responses to Time Pressures

It is highly predictable that busy people will stay busy no matter what. That is what they want and that is fine. What the brightest and busiest people do is to always be open to alternatives to doing what they do. They are: "Still spinning their top, but spinning it differently." They still stay very busy as that is what they and you want. Adding alternatives about "how to do things" makes you more likely to be more successful.

Using "I'm too busy" as a reason to not do something moves you away from satisfying relationships and the joy of achievement.

Instead, offer this. "I'm very busy right now with _____. I hear you want _____. I will or will not consider that later on. Let's talk more about this on _____." That is one assertive response that protects what you are presently doing while leaving the opportunity to engage in something else that may benefit you and others open and active. If you don't want to respond to the request, it gives you that opportunity as well.

Accordingly there is a well-known saying that goes like this: "If you want something done, asks a busy person to do it!" What enables them able to accomplish something when others would not do as well?

Professional time management experts help people take different approaches to their twenty-four hours so that less effort is expended, better results are obtained and they end up feeling more positive about their work. They also help companies which are having trouble "making it" when others in the same situation do not struggle as they are using time management principles and strategies at high levels.

A consumption driven civilization brings to all people stress and pressure. A change in the way you process this pressure allows people to learn new approaches not utilized before, adding new overall knowledge. This then helps you adjust attitudes, and results in people behaving differently. With that behavior change, their feelings are apt to change as well.

Three "Too Busy" Examples.

Let's determine which of the following situations have real pressures to their agendas in comparison with ones with hidden agendas, called mythical situations. Here are three examples. Readers can decide for themselves if they seem real or mythical.

(1) Sudan is the semi-retired bread winner in the family; he and his wife barely make it through the month on his pension, his paycheck from his weekend job at WaWa and her pension. One Friday, his wife was in a car accident on the way home and suffered enough kidney damage to put her in the hospital for five days. Her doctors provided excellent care and she was able to come home on Tuesday. Only then does Sudan call his sons to tell them what has happened to

their mother. They are furious with their Dad when they get the news and demand to know why he didn't call. His answer, "I was too busy," does not go over well with them. Real or mythical?

(2) Johan and Lowell are good friends and have been for some time. Over the years, they do a lot of things together. Each initiates time together, but lately Johan has been doing more leading in the relationship. He will suggest something for the two to do, but Lowell is frequently lukewarm to the idea and typically drags his feet at doing his part or shows up late when they are due to go somewhere. He always apologizes, saying, "I'm sorry, I am just so busy," and tells Johan about his busy day. An example is when the two of them plan to go get a load of mulch after work with Johan's pickup truck and Lowell shows up an hour and a half late. "I'm sorry; I just got busy with other things," he says as usual. Another time Lowell suggests that the two of them take a canoe trip down a small nearby stream, something they use to do often. He says he will bring the canoe. He shows up on time for this planned trip. Although surprised, Johan is happy to see his friend, but then finds himself commenting on how it is so unlike Lowell to be on time. Upon hearing that, Lowell drives off mad, leaving Johan home alone. Real or mythical?

(3) Susan is a 24-year-old single woman who works as a buyer for a national department store. She is often 15-30 minutes late to work because she has to walk her dog, stop by and see her seventy-five year-old mother, or her old car won't start. She always apologizes, saying, "I get up early but I have too many things to do in the morning to always come in at the same time." She is a good employee overall, but her team members never know whether she will make their three times a week 8:30 a.m. planning meeting. It does make for bad feelings often. Real or mythical?

The Answers Are . . .

Actually, all three are mythical. They are what they are but they don't have to be what they are. In the first example, there clearly is something else going on with Sudan. He had five twenty-four hour days to call his sons. What are factors in his relationship with his sons? Is he so lost by having his wife in the hospital that he doesn't make any decisions? These are questions I would seek answers to before I would seek any change. One good thing comes out of the son's anger; Sudan now knows they care about him and his wife.

In the case of Johan and Lowell there is male competiveness along with a passive-aggressive response by Lowell. The sharing of leadership has gotten out of balance between the two. Lowell has been sending the message, "I don't feel good when you lead more often than I do," via his passive-aggressive behavior of always showing up late. He regrouped by organizing the canoe trip. Johan took a payback approach by commenting on his being on time; he needs to instead thank Johan for the great idea of their going on a canoe trip again and he could say "I like it when you come up with ideas for us to do." What is good is that they both still care about each other and want the relationship to continue. They just have had a bump-in-the-road.

In the last example, there are multiple persons needing Susan's help at the same time. They are (1) her mother, (2) her dog, and (3) the employees that she manages. Although this hasn't reached the crisis state yet, it will if she doesn't do something differently. It also is a multi-repeated situation which, if she is paying attention, is a heads-up warning for her and an opportunity to be pro-active. I wouldn't make any specific suggestions to Susan. I would just encourage her to be pro-active.

In all cases, the main players are claiming their behavior is appropriate by self-justification, an unacceptable approach.

*   *   *

Approaches to Time and Life Management

Dr. D. is back from his errands. What are some approaches to this concept of time and life management you'd like to see all people adopt?" Dr. D focuses, and then says: "Please add them one at a time to their knowledge/skill bank until you get your life in order.

- From our family unity approach, join all your offspring in some of their activities or join with the grandchildren in going to watch an activity together. If you are not invited, invite yourself. Is there an event when both your adult child, including spouse or partner, and their children can come to your home for dinner? Start where they are, especially as all members of that generation are going to be self-centered, and find a way to routinely, systematically, and regularly involve you with them. If you live many miles away, you can use Skype, Internet conferencing software or FaceTime if your smartphone is an Apple;

- Recognize how strong the push to be independent is in all human beings, especially with the eighteen to forty year olds. What is important is that that value be paired up with the value of interdependence. An interdependent approach is a 'win-win' for all the extended families of Emerging and Young Adults and their parents as they together deal with worldly pressures. The Latin phrase, 'quid pro quo' comes to mind;

- Enroll in a Yoga class and learn how to meditate and how to relax. Yoga teaches one how to gain self or individual control by giving up social control. This is very important for parents of eighteen to forty year-old adults and in other relationships where control has become a distancing factor;

There is a website that begins to discuss this approach with an article entitled, 'The Greatest Gift . . . Time.' http://www.bestofyoutoday.com/spirituality/greatest-gift-time;

- One of the secrets of life is that the purpose of life is not to work or achievement but to enjoy the art of 'being.' Value relationships over material possessions. Enjoy the journey as much as you do the destination. Winning at golf or being the saleswoman of the month is not as important as with whom you do these things."

Dr. D: "Change is so important for all of us. We described how extended family members could improve in many areas as they journey through life. I have offered explanations of the way things are and suggestions as what to do regarding them. In any case, there is always much more to learn. Goodbye."

© Dr. D.'s Domains 2013

Chapter Nine

Feeling and Valuing One's Way in Families

In the human house, good quality workmanship is assertive communication; poor quality workmanship is passive-aggressive communication. Good quality materials are relationships; bad quality materials are related to materialism.

You change values by focusing on the new ones that you want to add. In doing so, those get stimulated and give out rewards, which displace the old values. You avoid resentment feelings and learn how to turn the volume up on the new ones, which eventually becomes loud enough to drown out noise from the old values . . .

Dr. Dennis Cogswell

Look Beyond the Packaging
for the Real Product.

Dr. D. was at a place in Forever Family Complex where he knew no one would find him, except Judy Bearister. She didn't know where he was as she had never been there, nor likely knew that it existed. Dr. D. left her a map, instructions, and pass key for the elevator and, as long as she got off on the seventh floor, she would find her way here.

Dr. D. was sitting on the deck enjoying his morning coffee as the sun came up the mountain. He heard footsteps and was about to say, "Hi Judy," when another woman, about Judy's age, stuck her head out the deck door. She looked familiar to him, but he couldn't place her. "Oh well", he thought to himself, "I'll just wait and see how this one unfolds." To her he said: "Welcome, come and sit down."

The woman thanked him, but did not say who she was or how she got up here. She was well-dressed, appeared to be in her late fifties or early sixties, and she wore nice clothes including walking shoes. She looked around and moved over to the edge of the deck where there was a great view outward and downwards in which she quickly got lost.

He hadn't figured out how to talk to this woman when Judy Bearister made that choice for him. She came bouncing in and said: "Sorry I'm behind, had to stop at the little girl's room, so I sent Bernice up here to meet you. I see you two have gotten acquainted." They hadn't, but Bernice wasn't going to say that, so neither did Dr. D. He decided to go with the flow; in fact, he had to because he certainly wasn't in charge here.

Judy must have sensed something or it was her nature to summarize so she began. "Bernice is a long-time church friend. She and her husband have two boys and one girl, grown adult children now, about the same age as our three. All are married, at least sort of. I asked her to come so you could hear what was going on in their family that was of concern to all of us. Both John and I are at a complete loss for what to say to Bernice and her husband, Barney. Bernice, tell him about your kids. Share what you have shared with us. Focus on Gene, your youngest."

Bernice looked grateful to Judy but was still cautious with Dr. D. as they hadn't talked directly, of which Judy was unaware. Bernice began telling about all her two oldest married children, one daughter and one son, their spouses and their children. Judy quickly interrupted. "We are all proud of this side of your family, but this isn't what I brought you to tell. Go ahead and share about Gene, what a disappointment he is to your husband and my husband, John. Dr. D. will listen and know what to ask and say."

Bernice cried softly: "Judy, I can't. This is too hard for me to talk to someone that I don't know. I shouldn't be here . . . I will only stay if you explain it to him," motioning to Dr. D.

Judy thought quickly and knew Bernice wasn't bluffing and she would leave, although it is better for the one hurting the most to share, So she looked to Dr. D. for guidance. He thought quickly, again saying to himself go with the flow. He nodded to Judy to continue. "Gene, their youngest, is twenty-six and has a college degree and a good job. He dated some in college but seemed so career-oriented that they didn't worry about him not having a steady girlfriend. However, Gene now has really stunned his parents and, when it gets out; our whole church community will be in an uproar. Gene has just told his parents that he is married and that children are on the way. This was a great enough shock, but he then went to the car and got his love to introduce to his parents, and his spouse is a man! His name is Franklin and the two of them got married several weeks ago in a ceremony in Franklin's home state where single sex marriage is legal. They were honeymooning when Bernice and her husband thought their son was just vacationing. Gene and Franklin want children and see no reason to wait[16]. They have started adoption procedures in Franklin's state, a process that currently takes nine months. Gene knew that there would be some questions but didn't expect the reaction he got. His father, Barney, stormed out of his home and went off somewhere. Bernice didn't know where that was until John Bearister called and told Bernice that Barney and he were in a downtown bar, drinking to the good old days. Barney would only come home after he knew that Gene and 'that man' were gone. He won't acknowledge what has occurred; a baby is going to be here in nine months. I don't know

---

[16] As with heterosexual couples, the recommendation, even for a couple who has been living together, is to wait 9-12 months before starting a family. The two persons need to experience the marital relationship before the nature dynamics of adding a third person to the marriage come into play.

what I think . . . Dr. D., I know Barney and Bernice didn't rise their kids this way, what could they have done wrong? What can they all do now?"

Dr. D. responded immediately. "Bernice, is it ok if Judy holds your hand?"[17] Judy did not need any instruction or prompting to take Bernice's hand.

Dr. D. continued: "I will do several things for you today. You will be given a lot. It will take some listening and discussing with Judy and then with another counselor before you are comfortable. Judy will explain to you that I do not presently see clients or families here at The Forever Family Complex. Instead, I will help you find a good professional that will help you beyond today. Here is a column we have written about finding a professional counselor, along with five names of those that we know have vacancies. Share it with Judy, make a call right away for an appointment, and then take it home to share with Barney."

Both Bernice and Judy seemed to being feeling better and Bernice mouthed a thank-you to Dr. D. He saw and acknowledged that. He then said: "Let me summarize what I have heard about you and your husband and your extended family. You two clearly value loving relationships, having a stable and long existing family, value church and God, having a strong work ethic and want your adult offspring to be able to support themselves right out of college.

---

[17] If he had known Bernice well, Dr. D. would have touched her briefly as she really needed that support. But he didn't know her at all. He also had Judy, who was a close friend. Bernice would react quite positive to Judy's touch. In fact, both Bernice and Judy would benefit from that that comes from holding hands.

"It is important that you, Bernice, put on new glasses to examine what you have with your children, because you can be loving and so proud of all three of them . . . Yes, including Gene."

But how, we didn't know he was gay. We didn't raise him that way. What are others going to think?" stuttered Bernice.

Dr. D. knew this was hard to handle. Very patiently, he repeated himself, looking directly into Bernice's eyes. "Bernice, put on these new glasses. They actually follow your lifelong prescription; things just look different in the frames, on the outside. Where it counts, they are exactly what you and Barney taught your children to seek. It just so happened that with Gene, he chose a much less conventional frame in which to display his choices. Let me explain. Your oldest two kids are both married; so is Gene. Your oldest two kids are in love with their spouses and show that to you and your husband. So is Gene. They all either have kids or plan to do so. Gene and Franklin state clearly that they want children, several, in fact, although they have to adopt. I think you are aware that Judy's oldest is adopted and she is more than fine with that. She can tell you all about that. Gene and Franklin are going to make you grandparents once more and they, and their kids, are going to need grandparents.[18] Your two oldest kids and their spouses all work and

---

[18] The adoption process is a very sound one. It is designed to help needy children find families, not needy parents to find children. Thus the process is very specific and inclusive. One requirement for both a heterosexual couple, and a gay couple, is that they will have to demonstrate quality of relationship and that the relationship will last. In either case, a child will not be able to be adopted until the relationship has passed the test of time. If all goes well, Gene and Franklin will be married over two years before the decision to place a child with them is made. Then, they are evaluated for a nine-month period as to whether they are meeting the child's needs. That is from where the nine-month idea came.

work hard. So do Gene and Franklin. Trust that he chose a good mate in Franklin who will also learn to love you."

Bernice: "I hear you and I will think about this that way. This is not what any of us expected. Yet, this feels so strange."

Dr. D. "I know that. The feelings you are having now are quite normal and will change as you change your thinking. That is the way it works with feelings, not the other way around.

"Having a son have another man as a marital partner is quite different from what you and your oldest two did, and most of the church members' kids did. But Gene and Franklin are not the first to make this choice, nor are they abnormal. They are just different."

Judy joins in. "Remember when we went to see Gene in his first apartment at the start of his junior year and he had gone there to paint and clean it before he showed it to his parents? Remember your reaction to the deep purple he chose for the living room. That was a shock. Remember how you were surprised that Barney wasn't shocked at the color and, in fact, went over to the paint can, read the ingredients and said: 'Gene, the color isn't what I expected, but I didn't expect you to buy the great quality paint you did either. This is really quality paint. Look how it feels, covers in one coat and the luster to it. Wow son, give me five!'"

*   *   *

Family Values and Feelings.

Dr. D., Bernice and Judy continued to talk for about 30 minutes with Dr. D. repeating the same information but shortening and focusing it each time. Bernice began to feel better and think differently. She realized that she might adjust, but what about

Barney? Both Dr. D. and Judy said that once she found a good counselor that she liked, the counselor would help her know how to approach Barney about joining her at the appointments.

Different marital configurations have been a part of the American family scene for centuries. During Aristotle and Plato's time, many of their community leaders were gay and no one saw that as bad. The term "homosexuality" didn't appear in the American language until the 1930s when it was introduced by religious organizations. In actuality the organization of today's family is similar to the organization of the pre-industrial family. Post-industrial families became more private, nuclear, and domestic and based on the emotional bonding between husband and wife, and between parents and children. Today, as it always has been, families are based on values and value conflict and/or feeling conflict are a chief cause of family disunity (Walsh, 1999). The strength of a family entails its values of unity, structure (a family is not democratic, never was, never will be), familiar roles, and the ability to adapt but not abandon itself in changing times. Extended families are about communication, feelings, and relationships.

A Brief History of Family Values

In our country, the concept of "family values" means different things to different people. The first is that they are beliefs we hold individually that come from societal beliefs. Secondly, it is the family of birth or of origin that is most valued, even though that nuclear family only lasts about twenty years. The phrase "family values" actually came about in the 20th century from social and religious conservatives who needed it for political means. The intent has been to claim that the world has seen a decline in family values since the end of the Second World War. That claim is untrue.

The family is valued as much if not more than before. What has changed are some of the features and structure of the family.[19]

From this conservative point of view, we pride ourselves on being a Christian country, although we have a very diverse religious population. We often don't behave like a Christian country, but then again, that depends on one's view. Even those who declare themselves to be "non-Christian", either because they have a different set of religious beliefs or no religious beliefs at all, recognize that Christian values are viewed as the main values. In 1998, a Harris survey found that fifty-two percent of women and forty-two percent of men thought that *family values* meant "loving, taking care of, and supporting each other". Thirty-eight percent of women and thirty-five percent of men thought *family values* meant "knowing right from wrong and having good values". Two percent of women and one percent of men thought of *family values* in terms of the "traditional family". Ninety-three percent of all women thought that society should value all types of families. Questions about family values have generally included issues concerning the current diversity of family structures. (Unknown, 2011).

How does one go about changing a family value to a different one that is desired? The answer lies in contact, contact, contact; exposure and time spent with a person who has those new values. In the case at the beginning of this chapter, Bernice and Barney

---

[19] The world outside of our family can certainly bring grief to families when its values are in opposition. Many religions think that being in a serious, loving and even a marital relationship with a member of the same gender is a sin. However, that can vary from church to church and minister to minister with the same denomination. Catholic families follow Catholic belief, dogma, and structure very well, except when they choose not to. A good example is birth control, which the church officially opposes, but the majority of many women of child bearing age, chooses to follow. This is always a tough choice, but it will be made and is being done so over and over today.

would need to spend time with Gene and Franklin, starting off with visiting the couple in their home. One other venture would be to visit Franklin's parents to see what they had (have) in common with Barney and Bernice. In all cases, it will not help anyone if there is any hiding of feelings. It is ok to share any feelings, as long as they are owned as demonstrated in the chapter on assertiveness. Feelings will be the last thing to change, preceded by the values, the information one has about the subject. In this case, the more everyone knows about each other, especially in relation to one's strengths, the better things will be. One always changes best from a strength perspective. Remember these two truisms: (1) In the world we live in, feelings trump facts or information and values trump feeelings; and (2) Feelings don't change first; instead, behavior or thoughts must change first, followed by feelings. Eventually, new feelings will replace the old ones.

A Review of Feelings and Especially Their Causes

One most commonly claimed feeling is guilt, although it isn't a feeling at all but a judgment that you have done something that violates your internal values.; To help you comprehend guilt, "It" is waiting to share what has happened to "It", who is quite innocent of all charges. The most prevailing one is to blame "It" for causing almost everything to happen, especially feelings. Often family members blame "It" for what comes from them. Here is "Its" self-defense, with expert after expert, including the Forever family, waiting to testify. Perhaps finally, the general public will hear and learn the truth!

* * *

I'm Innocent: I Don't have the Power to Cause Feelings in You.

Poor me, "It's having a bad day". I often have a bad day as "It" is blamed for everything. In a chapter on communication, "It" is blamed for "having the last word." Today, "It" is blamed for causing all feelings, as in "It makes me so mad . . ." or "That's 'it', I have had it with . . ." Almost everyone thinks that feelings come from others when that is not true at all. This mistaken view is so strong that people will actually blame others and "It" for their negative feelings, but then seldom gives "It" credit for their positive ones. Well, I am writing to tell you, "It" isn't that way at all!!!

Experts who think a lot about feelings have figured out that a given feeling comes or originates from within the person feeling it. Even with that understanding people still wonder what causes that feeling because people just don't live in a vacuum; there are other people around us almost hourly. The reality is that feelings do not just occur by themselves. Feelings are felt when something happens that stimulates a feeling to appear. Or, they are influenced by another's feelings, behavior or values to appear. "Influenced" is quite different than "caused". e.g. if someone behaves badly towards two people the same age, gender, race, occupation, and more who are standing side-by-side with no differences in location, one person may feel angry while the other does not. The second person may have another feeling or none at all. If that badly behaving person is REALLY causing the anger, why then don't both people feel angry?

A related explanation may help. "There is a correlational or common relationship between the event and the feeling, which means that the event and the feeling share something in common. One doesn't cause the other; they just both occur one immediately after the other."

There is no cause and effect relationship. We are influenced or conditioned by the behavior, values or feelings of others to then feel a certain feeling. e.g. when other people behave badly this influences our reaction, which is often negative and makes life seem difficult. Then we respond with our feelings to what was done with/to us as a reaction to but not caused by, what came from the other person or event. Our feelings will often then take over, but all feelings start or arise from within us. This is what happens, no matter what people typically claim happens.

"It" also wants all to know, (All is a friend), that when you comprehend how this works, it provides an opportunity to do something about the situation in which you find yourself and even be influential on another's behavior. It gives you options to influence things to go in a positive direction that you do not have with the old and wrong beliefs. Again, until "It" is heard, not blamed, there may be a lot of misinformation prevalent and other people still believing the myth and blaming "It."

That's enough for now. I'm tired but glad to have an opportunity to take the blame away from "It".

* * *

The Feeling Track Down Process

Feelings are the emotional and physical responses humans have to what they think about and are reactions to daily events. Because humans are different, we respond differently to the above, but with the same feelings. What one person gets angry about doesn't even bother another person. Later on, the second person has the similar angry feelings but to a different stimulus.

One can either think about one's feelings e.g. "I am angry I have to go to my new job tomorrow." or one can directly feel them e.g.

"Darn it, I have to go to that new job tomorrow!" The latter is preferred but not always. When one is in a difficult place with a set of feelings, start recognizing what goes with them. Tell yourself that the feelings are really real, but the consequences of the feelings may not be. After you have carried out this process, which we call "Feeling Track Down", then give yourself permission to discharge those feelings. Sometimes that is best done through using feeling words. Other times a good cry or a physical workout works best. Here is an exercise that you can use to think about and through your feelings. Just fill in the blanks.

Today I feel _____ because I _____.

I was _____ (scared, angry, anxious, etc.) when I _____ so I _____.

In order to feel better when I feel _____, I _____.

A Common Occurrence: Family Appeasement

In all relationships, from dealing with a temper tantrum of a two-year-old to dealing with a hostage situation to dealing with a temper tantrum of a forty-year-old uncle in an extended family, it is a big "NO-NO" to give in to that sudden and intense expression of emotion that has a hook connected to it. The hook is that the individual feeling wants something done their way, hasn't been able to get it that way through normal means, so has intense emotions that they believe are threatening to another person so that person) use them as leverage to work to get their ways. Most of us know of the four-year-old in the grocery store who wants some candy but Mom says "No", so the youngster throws his/herself down on the floor and starts yelling and kicking. Mom is in a very tough spot there because she is initially embarrassed about not having control of her child and also how it disrupts others shopping. If she gives

121

into the youngster, it will only happen again. The same thing is true of forty-year-old Uncle Lewis who is single and wanted to have alcohol at your anniversary party. He is told "no" and he leaves, reappearing well after the beginning time, and comes drunk, bringing in his own beer and says that he will just sit here quietly and watch and drink. The tendency is to give into Uncle Lewis, just like it is to give into Little Lewis. Perhaps that is what happened and is why Uncle Lewis still has temper tantrums?

The response recommended is different from that offered by friends. We suggest that you first tell four-year-old Lewis or forty-year-old Lewis that you recognize what he is feeling and acknowledge that feeling, describing what you think it is and how bad he must be feeling. Repeat this until you know that they have heard you.

Then, tell what comes next, as clearly as you can and follow through with it. With Little Lewis, once you know he is not hurting anyone, himself, or store merchandise, say: "I'm going over here two aisles away and turn my back on you. You will be able to see me. Calm you down and I will come back and we will finish our shopping and _____." (Do not give him any food as a reward, even "good" food). This may take many times, with repeating the instructions, until it works. The parent that is being coerced must set the rules and leave until the child complies. If Mom is the one the tantrum is directed towards, then she sets the rules and if Dad is in the store, he comes over and stands on the other side, two aisles away, to make sure Little Lewis doesn't hurt others or store merchandise. Yes, to you it might seem very embarrassing to let little Lewis continue to tantrum with others watching. Most people are watching but are in support taking the right steps. It will only be the uninformed who complain about being inconvenienced; they don't know what you know. Once it is clear that either Big or Little Lewis has heard you, follow the same pattern for both.

With Big Lewis, someone must take him firmly by the handor shoulder and escort him outside the house and off the property. He then is sent home, saying "You must go home to stop drinking. We will see you later."[20]

Dr. D's. Famous Summary

Dr. D. "Sometimes the best words are no words. I don't want to take away from any of the above so will only add: "We have offered what we know; Remember, there is always more to learn."

© 2013 Dr. D.'s Domains

---

[20] The specific choice of words is so important. What is offered here is what is to be said, as in following a script. It would be a mistake to say something like: "I know not getting candy now is making you sad." Or "I know not being able to drink beer at this party is making you angry." In both cases, you are suggesting that the rule they don't like is causing the negative emotion. Nothing could be more incorrect. Little Lewis and Adult Lewis are both causing their own negative emotions and must be helped to learn how to control them. If you let them blame others, this bad behavior will continue.

Chapter Ten

Ups and Downs:
Which Way to Go To Change[21]

Some Truisms: Borrowed and Re-worked.

If you always do what you always did,
you will always get what you always got.

In order to get somewhere, you have to go somewhere.

In order to go somewhere, you have to move something.

Talk is cheap and easy to come by.
Change takes effort and action.

It is now time to "walk the walk" rather than just "talk the talk."

Dr. Dennis Cogswell

The Mobius Strip Approach to Conflict

John Bearister arrived to a dark conference room. He first wondered if he had the date or time mixed up but then remembered running into Dr. D. yesterday when both said they were looking Foreword to today's meeting. He knew Kelly must be there as the smell of coffee was everywhere. He decided to wait and to seek out

---

[21]   The answer to the Title question is "Up", if you can. This is based on the belief of building on the positive or always moving towards what you want rather than running away from what you don't want. It does depend on many factors, however. On a hike it is hardier on your lungs to go up a hill, but what a good feeling when you do. Coming down, it is actually harder on your knees and ankles, so that too is a challenge.

a cup of the Java to further wake him up . . . Soon he heard the sound of footsteps and thought that it must be Dr. D. It was.

"Sorry I'm late, John. The weight room manager had a family emergency and was twenty minutes late opening up this morning. I insist to myself on exercising regularly so did my full routine . . . I see you have found the coffee?"

"Kelly as usual makes a lot of coffee and makes it well. I want to start off right away with the calls I have received." Dr. D. motioned John to continue. John does just that.

"Rex and Rhonda, two family friends, have always had a tumultuous marriage, all thirty years of it. Since their last daughter got married this summer, they have done nothing but fight. Rex calls me and complains; Rhonda calls Judy and does the same. We don't want to do anything with them both now, which they really need, as they keep fighting the same battles over and over. What can be said to them or what can Judy and I do? We don't want to stop our friendship . . ."

Dr. D. reaches into his briefcase and pulls out a small strip of paper in a loop with one twist in it. "I have something that you can take home with you, share with Judy, then you can make two more copies and take them to your friends. It is called a Mobius Strip or Mobius Band. Its surface has only one side and no end. It was designed independently by two German mathematicians, August Ferdinand Mobius and Johann Benedict Listing, in 1858. We have just adopted it as a part of our Families Are Forever Logo. Here is a picture of one on our website, our business cards, and everywhere we can think of to show it.

TheFamilyForever

John nodded: "I know the logo but didn't know what it represents." Dr. D. then continues.

"How this fits Rex and Rhonda is that they are still trying to win old, old arguments. I'm thinking they often say, 'you started it when you . . .'"

John: "That is exactly what happens. How does this deal with that pattern?"

Dr. D. knew how to explain this well. "The Mobius Strip has no beginning nor any end. That is what likely true about their arguments is. Both want to prove that the other started the argument and that the other is responsible for their present problems but they never do. Just like this Mobius Strip, their arguments have no beginning nor any end. They go on forever . . . To help them move from this infinity-based argument, here is what I ask that Judy and you do. As hard as it may be, you both are to go over to their house when you know they are both there, you don't need an invitation. Take them each one of these and tell them that they have been arguing for years and nobody knows nor cares who started what. Neither you, nor I, nor Mobius. Tell them emphatically that you want them to stop any discussion of the past and that you two will help them move on."

Learning Golf's Life Lessons

"The second step comes out of the fact that you play golf with Rex, and Judy plays golf with Rhonda. Both of you are to take a recent scorecard from a round for each of them that shows their score with you to their house. Ask them the question: 'How did you come up with such a good score?' Do not let them in any way discount that score by saying, 'Well, that wasn't my best round' . . . or 'I'm still not putting well.' Those are examples of the negative scorekeeping that they are doing in their marriage. Don't share that yet, but talk with each of them together, asking then to describe what they did well in that round. You may have to work hard to get there. Focus on their strengths, as a counselor will do with them when they start counseling. Take turns, Judy and John, with this explanation, making sure you two are speaking with one voice. They won't get it as well as you do at first, but that is OK. For now, all they have to do is to hear you. If necessary, repeatedly ask them: 'Rex or Rhonda, what do you hear us saying?' Repeat, question, repeat, until all are at least on the same hearing page.

"Remember, both Rex and Rhoda are getting some reward by being able to talk to you two about the other's negatives. You two are going to have to agree that you will no longer listen to their complaints but only about what they like about each other. You will have to explain that to them, again speaking with one voice. To soften the blow that they may think this is, tell them that they are much closer together than they realize as they are both fighting the exact same way."

Knowing that too much instruction leads to confusion, Dr. D. ends. "Then tell them this. Just like you go to golf pro at the country club to get help with a hurdle you can't get over, I am going to ask you to go to a professional counselor, both of you together. Just as the pro is likely to tell you first what he likes about your swing, the professional counselor is going to help the two of you deal from strength on your marital swing or relationship. Here again you may have to help them by saying that Judy and you will go with them to their first joint session, and even into the session with them. Once you get them there and they have made contact with the counselor, you two will want to leave. Go somewhere together, Judy and John, and celebrate your marriage and what good friends you are to Rex and Rhonda."

John is beaming. "That's amazing Dr. D. That is just what I wanted from you. I think they will hear us as the two of them love golf and we think they still love each other. I didn't know that if a couple fights a lot but each fights the same way as the other, that instead of things being bad, they are trying to stay together. The worse thing is if a couple is not talking at all to each other."

Dr. D. smiles, nods in agreement to John and walks him to the door. John leaves, as he need to do, and asks Dr. D. if he may call him after they do this. He doesn't even wait for the answer but hurries home wanting to tell Judy what they can do to help their good friends. He is relieved.

Dr. D. starts reading and enjoying the end of his coffee. He knows he was helpful and that he is not needed by John anymore today.

*   *   *

Truisms Can Guide Change

The quotes at the very beginning of the chapter, from famous people and my own pen can be called truisms, sayings or beliefs that a lot of people in a particular group or country believe to be true. They may also be statements that some people believe important. Truisms themselves do not have lengthy or detailed definitions because they are not evaluated to be true by definition. Instead they should be viewed as an argument that is considered to be true by the vast majority of people; Thus, most people believe that a truism offered is not disputable.

The point of these truisms, which are fun to say over and over again, is to guide change. Period. The same old path is the same old path. People who still want to be influential with their adult offspring and/or friends are most successful when they have multiple methods and techniques to utilize in the varied and challenging situations they find in their lives.

Change is not easy, and it seems that the older one gets, the harder it is to change, although I don't have any research to back that up. Those who think deeply about these things offer three learning points: (1) All people resist change; (2) change is inevitable; and (3) people change the best from strength, not from being corrected, certainly not from bullying, nor when someone says: "You are always hammering at me." We call the latter "negative scorekeeping," which is a favorite pastime of Americans. Let's look at these one at a time.

"All people resist change." We humans like things to go well and seek out homeostasis or a standing still condition. Since the concept homeostasis came from biology, let's take a look at this medical example. We like to be healthy. Our bodies try to maintain our health but eventually break down. Going online to Wikipedia, the free encyclopedia, usually is quite helpful. It has something to say about everything. According to the following quote, every illness has aspects to it that are a result of lost homeostasis:

> Just as we live in a constantly changing world, so do the cells and tissues survive in a constantly changing microenvironment. The "normal" or "physiologic" state then is achieved by adaptive responses to the ebb and flow of various stimuli permitting the cells and tissues to adapt and to live in harmony within their microenvironment. Thus, homeostasis is preserved.

> It is only when the stimuli become more severe, or the response of the organism breaks down, that disease results—a generalization as true for the whole organism as it is for the individual cell." (Robbins, 1984).

Author George Leonard, in his 2010 book, ***The Keys to Success and Long Term Fulfillment***, discusses how homeostasis affects our behavior and who we are. He states that homeostasis will prevent our body from making drastic changes and maintain stability in our lives even if it is detrimental to us. For example, when an obese person starts exercising, homeostasis in the body resists the activity to maintain stability. Another example Leonard uses is an unstable family where the father has been a raging alcoholic and suddenly stops drinking and the son starts up a drug habit to maintain stability in the family. Homeostasis is the main factor that stops people changing their habits because our bodies view change as dangerous unless it is very slow. Leonard discusses this dilemma as the media today only encourages fast change and quick results." http://gettingstronger.org/2010/03/george-leonards-mastery/.

This first statement—that all people resist change—then is important for individuals to really comprehend. Just because a family member comes to you wanting to change doesn't mean that they will or that it is easy. Don't expect them to accept everything you have to offer or the suggestions that you make. Expect resistance. Know what to do to help people go about changing because they need your help as much in how to go about changing as what to change.

Change expert Dr. Stan Goldberg offers the "10 rules of change:" (1) All behaviors are complex; (2) Change is frightening; (3) Change must be positive; (4). Being is easier than becoming; (5) Slower is better; (6) Know more, do better; (7) Change requires structure; (8) Practice is necessary; (9) New Behaviors must be protected; and (10) Small success are big. (http://www.psychologytoday.com/articles/200210/the-10-rules-change)."

"All behaviors are complex" relates well to our Forever Families' principle of multiple causation; there is always more than one factor that influences something to be the way that it is. With families, it is both the complexity of today's work world and the pressure/expectation to be better than your parents e.g. make more money, live in bigger house, that results in stress for Emerging Adults. In order for change, both of these two influences must be addressed.

No, Not Negative Score Keeping Again[22]

Points two and three can be approached as one point. Even though we naturally resist change, it is inevitable. We also recognize that people change the best from strength. People always want to "negatively score keep" so we start there for several reasons, one being that that is where they want to start. However, what that gets you is an understanding of what is wrong. That's all. There still are other steps needed to produce change. If you spend all your time talking about what is wrong, you will never get to what you want and what to do to get there. Many change models advocate spending little time on the problem and most of your counseling time on what is wanted (goals) and how to get there (strategies). One model goes as far as saying: "You don't need but a minute to state what is wrong; take three minutes to focus on what is wanted."

The point here is to set goals about what one wants to achieve in positive terms, not what one wants to not have anymore. e.g.

---

[22] This where one pays attention only to mistakes made rather than starting with success and then looking at what didn't happen. Actually all major sports do it right. e.g. football, our real national pastime, does give out penalties but they are not computed in the final score. What is computed in the final score are your team's accomplishments and the team with the highest score, wins.

"I want to lose weight" is not a good change statement; "I want to weigh 210 pounds by the end of the month" is a good change statement. "I want our family to stop fighting with each other" is both vague and focuses on the past or what is wrong. "I want our family to have two discussions a day with each other on a common issue where both state what they heard the other one say" is a better change statement. It is important that the change is not giving something up but is adding a new behavior or doing something different. It is important that vague language e.g. "We have to get along better" be replaced with "I want to hear twice a day when you like something I do." With vague language the speaker may know what s(he) means (although often not), but others will disagree as to what is being said. Family members need to talk in specific ways using behavioral language.

Change requires structure and practice is necessary are two important points. A structure for change involves having goals, which answer the question "what." The best goals are then broken down into sub-goals or objectives, stated in behavioral terms, are measurable and dated. "I want to lose weight" is marginally OK for a goal. A good objective might be "'By Saturday, April 9, I will weigh 185 pounds." That is easily measurable in a way that can't be easily misunderstood or sabotaged. Go to a good set of scales and weigh yourself works here. Finally, find a way to offer or obtain evidence that the goal is or is not being met. Evidence is defined as something that is tangible and able to be viewed by all. In this weight example, evidence would be to keep a chart of weekly weigh-ins and to bring that to each counseling session.

Changing Feelings, Values and/or Attitudes, Thoughts and Behaviors

What people often want to change is their feelings because that is what they believe causes the most trouble for them. The simplest approach to helping change feelings is "the discharge strategy."

Feeling or emotions always seek to be discharged. When a person's feelings have been discounted, or not allowed by another person, the first person tends to repress or story their negative feelings instead of directly expressing them. The term "directly expressed" is important because feelings will be discharged; that is their nature and they are relentless to that end. If not verbally expressed, feelings will be acted out or expressed via other symptoms, called psycho-somatic symptoms. Delayed grief reactions are a good example of this. Unfortunately, all humans will experience loss. It is part of the human experience. Many people think that this happens first when we are born and leave the warmth and safety of our mother's body.[23] Often just being a good listener is enough to help a person change their feelings. Your active listening gives others permission to feel and the natural cachexia process does the rest. However, most often, different interventions are needed. A more advanced process is to recognize that thoughts drive feelings or values. Thus we have to work in the affective or feeling domain to get the wanted results. Cognitive psychology takes this approach and has much to offer on what to do and how to go about it. (http://psychology.about.com/od/psychotherapy/a/cbt.htm)

People everywhere believe that their behavior will or can change AFTER their feelings change, yet it is just the opposite that works. When we help people change their behaviors, their feeling follow. For example, depressed people say: "when I feel better, I'll get back to my regular routine and go out with you" when it is just the opposite sequence that will work. Counselors working

---

23   Theorists go on to say this automatically results in some separation anxiety. The amount of is often used), then the anxiety will go away. However, if the baby is placed on a cold cart and taken off to be weighed, and measured, this may not happen. It is important for prospective parents to think through in detail what does happen, both to mother and baby, once the delivery of the new arrival is complete and to arrange for that to actually happen. However, one will also run into hospital protocol and this will have to be negotiated.

with depressed people seek to get the clients to DO something as many things as possible. They start with small items like "read the newspaper each day by 10 a.m." or "talk with your mother on the phone for at least 15 minutes twice a day, no matter how you feel."

Changing values or the attitudes that come from the values domain is the hardest change to make. Values guide our lives/behaviors so we don't have to logically think through every situation, factor and opportunity that we face. They develop very early on and get reinforced by so many factors, including other persons and collective society. The toys one buys one's baby and whether one reads to the baby influence much, including value development. What parents and grandparents emphasize in relationships is noticed and remembered by the young child for future use.

In general, values are not good or bad; they simply are. What is not good is when someone has no established values or they are so different than the rest of the culture in which they live.

Most Americans value young children and seek to protect them. Pedophiles do not. At the moment the shooter in Connecticut went into the Sandy Grove Elementary School, he was not in touch with his given value system. Most Americans value human life and cannot easily kill another human being. When most policemen shoot someone in the line of duty, they are immediately put on administrative leave for two reasons. The first is to investigate if the taking of life was necessary. The second is to help them adjust to having killed another human being. Killing another human being is a difficult process to accept even though it was done in the line of duty as their personal values were violated. This latter reason is one major reason that placing armed volunteers in schools may have disastrous side effects for anyone of them who heroically save others only to suffer themselves from their killing another human being to save other's lives.

A person born and raised in a small town may have limited experience with any diversity. Their values then will correspond to their life experiences. To change those values, or add new ones, will only come about via repetitive new experiences. That is what influenced our old policy of bussing our children to different communities to go to school. It was to force interaction between diverse populations that would not happen automatically. The same problem is happening now with all the gated communities where people go to protect themselves and spend a great amount of time with those just like themselves. Both are quite natural happenings, universal, yet with un-thought through consequences for all. The values of independence and self-determination come into conflict with the value of interdependence and broad community interrelatedness, with no easy answers.

There is a very easy way to spot when you or someone else is valuing and that is to listen to the person's language. If they are using any of these words: "should", "should not", "must", "must not", "need to", "need not to" and/or "ought" & "ought not" then they are expressing a value. There is a difference between the statements: "You should lose weight" and "A lot of your health problems are because of your weight."

Most of our values are learned early in life and reinforced or relearned and relearned. That is one reason why they are so difficult to change. When my values are identified as being active, I call them "voices" or "parent tapes," which is an analogy to which most people can relate. One using this model then says to family members such things as: "I am hearing your voices here;" or "Your voices are really talking hard to you now."

To help someone actually change a value is a complicated process. One goal could be to add a value that would eventually replace another. One does so by helping people have new experiences that provide the opportunity to experience something that has not been experienced before. The bottom line is that "repetitive new experiences is the main way to change values." This belief goes against most punishment approaches that reinforce the old behaviors by focusing on trying to remove them; that well—intended approach results in more of the same. The violent crime rate typically goes up in the geographic area where and when a public execution occurs, not down as is the intent.

With families, value change is slower than with individuals as the many members in the family typically automatically combine to resist change. Even when it seems that family members differ so much by seeing them argue all the time, the opposite may be true. If each person in an argument is using the same process with the same intensity, they are actually quite close together in their coping behaviors. That can be good and re-directed to the family's advantage, or negative if the members reinforce each other to resist change. In almost all cases, the guiding hand of a third party is necessary to produce value change. That guiding hand can be a professional, such as a family minister, doctor or counselor, or a senior family member who understands the valuing process. It even can be a new granddaughter who brings an arguing family together to care for her or to enjoy her love of life.

*   *   *

As this chapter ends, we use our electronic communication capacity to hear from Dr. D. He is somewhere outside but near enough to still receive our signals. Let's call him and see.

Dr. D. soon responds and comes on screen. "Hi folks. I am right outside our complex where we have many wild blueberries, my favorite fruit. I am picking them for all to eat, but it is going slow because I am sampling every bush . . . of course, to make sure that they are ripe." . . . He pauses to smile to himself at his humor. "You all are finishing up talking about change. We have offered a lot and yet there is so much more that can be said. I hope that happens for you in other chapters. For now, take what you have and experience it. We have offered it for that purpose and hope that what is offered is helpful. Remember, there is always more to learn. Goodbye from the berry patch."

© 2013 Dr.D.'s Domains

Chapter Eleven

Contact. Relationship. Excitement:
A Continuous Cycle

Human beings must have action;
and they will make it up if they cannot find it.

Dr. Albert Einstein

As far as family goes, I would rather have a family member with
whom I fight than one who never talks to me. At least with a
'fighting family member' there is contact
and with contact, who knows what will happen?

Dr. Dennis Cogswell

Judy Barrister's 25,000 Pieces of Eight

Judy Bearister stuck her head in Dr. D.'s door and said: "Hi and surprise. I know you were expecting John, but I really need to talk with you and to do so alone. I will be right back."

That did indeed surprise Dr. D. It wasn't that Judy had not come alone before but that ending comment got his attention quickly. When she returned, he said, "Come on in and sit down. I see you have some of Kelly's coffee. She has switched to decaf so we all have switched, if you follow what I am saying?"

Judy had a hot cup, which she was already enjoying, so she didn't reply to Dr. D.'s commentary on The Forever Family Complex coffee politics. "I am sure glad to see you as I have had a big secret that I haven't told anyone in almost three months, no one, and I can't sit on it any longer. I had to come by myself so talked John into staying home. I haven't told him about my secret, although he isn't the issue. He will be shocked, like most people, but then he will quickly be happy. He will be hurt that I have been sitting on this, but he will get over it. Let me come right to the point. The problem is with my mother, sort of. It is best that I start from the beginning."

Dr. D.: "Yes, I am confused and curious about 'this secret.' Start from the beginning"

"Oh, the secret is really something. No one would ever guess it. I had a secret life, a fling, and a payoff I didn't expect. And now I have to do something about it . . . I think you are right; starting from the beginning is a good idea. I will do just that." Yet she pauses again and it is obvious that she will need some further prompting before saying anything.

"I'm listening. I bet this is good . . . you are OK, aren't you? You haven't done anything illegal or anything like that? I am quite clueless."

"You know my mother, Helen Modius, is 88 years young, living in a nice Lutheran assisted living facility in San Luis Obispo, California. That is my home town, where Daddy taught at Cal Polytechnic University, and where I went to college. Most kids want to go to college away from home, but not me. Why leave one of the prettiest places in America, in that part of California, and with a great university. Besides, I got free tuition." She pauses.

Dr. D. is beginning to lose it. All this is great, and he agrees with Judy about the beauty there, but what does this have to do with the big secret? Will she ever say?

Judy Bearister is a good storyteller but always too detailed. She senses Dr. D.'s frustration and thinks she had better do something about it. "Look, I hate dumping this on you when you didn't expect it. Perhaps I should just go and I'll figure it out myself." She got up to leave.

Dr. D.: "No, no, no. Leaving would be a terrible thing as I am still clueless. I mean it would be bad to keep this to yourself any longer. Just tell me what the secret is and then give the details."

"OK, here goes. I have a gambling problem. It's quite serious."

"Oh dear," says Dr. D., something he often says when concerned. When really concerned, he doubles or triples the "Oh, dear." Well, I am sure that we can help you with that. You know Gambler's Anonymous meets in our community room . . . In any case, explain a bit more."

Judy: "Thank you for not kicking me out. I go and see my mother about once every two months by flying from Denver to Las Vegas and then catching a regional jet into San Luis Obispo. I like visiting Mom; yet it is hard to get myself to schedule a trip. I always feel guilty when I am with her. She has always been critical of me, saying that she is just trying to help me reach my full potential. She is also very conservative. When we were growing up her church forbid card playing of any kind. We couldn't even play 'Old Maid' or that game where you say 'Oh ____', you know, cuss words, when you say the game's name. I think that is what the kids like about it . . . Oops." She sees him first. John, her husband, has just come into Dr. D.'s office.

"Hi everybody. I figured Judy was ready I stopped by here. We can go out to eat together for lunch. That is one of the great things about being a writer. I set my own hours. What are you chatting about?" John inquires, looking to one of the two to fill him in.

Dr. D. doesn't know what to say because he isn't sure what can be shared. And now with John here, Judy won't continue. "How she is going to talk her way out of this one?" he thinks to himself. He pauses and looks right at Judy as if to say: "OK, this is your mess, you deal with it."

Judy speaks to John. "Well, I was just talking with Dr. D. about San Luis Obispo, its great beauty, my going to college there. I didn't tell him that we met there, remember? I had just mentioned mother living there and you came in. I can stop and go to lunch with you. Dr. D., do you have any time this week that I can come and finish my story? I am feeling better."

Dr. D. wanted to say: "You may feel better but I am tied in knots. You tell me you have a secret, then a gambling problem, and then your husband comes in, who doesn't know your secret. You are all smiles to him and going to lunch with him and leaving me hanging. This all helps you feel better? I can't take any more of this avoidance, but how can I move you to talk? Now I have a secret too; I need a drink— some good red wine, something that is good for me because being a helping person isn't very good for me now." But he, of course, doesn't say that. Instead, he says out loud to both of them. "Yes, go have lunch. I can meet on Friday" and to himself, "you certainly have brought excitement into my life today, but I don't know what to do with it. "And then out loud, "I think I can make it to Friday. Can you come at 11 a.m. then?"

John and Judy are ready to leave hand in hand for lunch, and Judy says: "Yes, that will work. I hope you have plenty of excitement the rest of the week as I know what we talked about was pretty dull. I'll tell mother you send your best and we will talk again on Friday."

They leave and Dr. D. heads for his refrigerator where he has a bottle of Chateau Souverain, 2000 Sonoma County opened and chilled. That is the type of excitement he likes![24]

*   *   *

Excitement Demystified, A Bit.

Location, location, location is the key to a successful business. Relationship, relationship, relationship is the key to a successful family life. Contact, contact, contact is the essence of relationship. Excitement, excitement, and excitement is sought by all. Relationship, contact, and excitement all occur in the context of how we use time. Quite a while ago Dr. Eric Berne, after much observing of each of the above three and some deep thinking, concluded that there were clear ways we humans went about relationships and making contact. He related that to time usage and decided that the amount of human contact we sought had to do with the concept of excitement, especially at higher levels of relating. He called this upper level a human game.

That meant that there were rules of that relationship, but that they often were not the real rules or what one saw was not what one got. For example, in the basic game of checkers or chess, one may see an open avenue to capture the opponent's king or queen that seems to be left there by accident. Yet when the player moves to capture it, s(he) is tagged and eliminated by falling for this hidden trap set by the more skilled player. What excitement that is—to

---

[24] This wine won an award of Best Value Chardonnay of the Year with a blend pear, apple blossom and hazelnut accented by subtly smoky oak aromas. Read more: http://shareranks.com/9097,Best-California-Wines-Under-

trap another player and take advantage of their lack of awareness!
(Berne, 1971).

Low to Mid-level Games in Terms
of Excitement Generated

As we spend so much of our waking time at work for most of
our adult lives, some examples of games carried out or played at
work might help. For example, a vice president can play *Harried
Executive* on his job, saying "Yes" to so many requests that he
finally collapses. In the meantime, he harasses and overworks his
secretaries as well as himself. When Mr. Harried leaves the room,
his secretaries may stop their typing and filing activities and move
to a common pastime of *Ain't it Awful*. e. g. "That guy! He says
"Yes" to everybody, and we end up with a lot of extra work. Isn't
it awful?" When the boss re-enters the room, the secretaries may
either switch back to work activities or move to the ritual of a
coffee break or withdraw into their own fantasies, perhaps angry
ones, or initiate a game.[25]

A family-related game has to do with the human tendency to
look first and foremost at mistakes made rather than success
on individual variables. In families and elsewhere this is also
known as nitpicking. The definition of nitpicking is to criticize by
picking on small points. There is a difference between correcting
someone's writing mistakes by agreement to do so and seeking
things to criticize them on when you don't have a clear agreement
to do so. It is a way to "put the other down" or in his/her place.
Regular repeated nitpicking can become "haranguing," which
is long-standing, long lasting nitpicking that is more intense and
much more difficult to receive. If you want to criticize, the way

---

[25]   http://www.theadultchild.com/relationships-and-time-structuring-a-
typology.html

to do so is to first ask if you may share an opinion. Then, relate some positive aspects of the situation to balance his/her reaction, and seek to discuss what they heard you say, rather than have it just be a one-way communication. The discussion aids both the giver and the receiver and generally leads to a productive relationship on many levels.

Offering just a criticism without using the above procedure occurs often in families because there are many psychological rewards available. It is not hard to find a family member to nitpick you. It is an almost universal learned human response that when someone offers a new idea, one immediately tries to find out what is wrong with it instead of offering a more balanced response.

Other Views of Excitement

Others have researched and written about their views of excitement. Robert Pirsig, in his classic novel, **Lila**, writes about New York City and how it is such an exciting place to live and visit. He labels it a quality issue, resulting from both the chaos and stability of cities.

Another similar approach comes from theoretical physicist Geoffrey West in a 2010 **New York Times** column where he states:

> These are the laws, they say, that automatically emerge whenever people "agglomerate," cramming themselves into apartment buildings and subway cars. It doesn't matter if the place is Manhattan, New York or Manhattan, Kansas; the urban patterns remain the same . . . What we found are the constraints that describe every city . . . Cities can't be managed and that's what makes them so vibrant (West 2010).

*   *   *

A Brief Travelogue on The Big Apple

We have a Forever Family extended member calling in about her trips to the Big Apple and how she sees the City. She is Lisa Ann, and here is what she had to offer.

THE CITY: New York City

I love "the Big Apple" and have visited it ten times, including two to run in the New York City Marathon with another run canceled because the Marathon was cancelled due to the big storm. Usually I go with three-seven girlfriends, for a four-day "girl's weekend." We like Manhattan for its restaurants, shopping, and tourist attractions.

What has me being so enthralled about New York City (NYC)? Although I live in a city myself, New York is one of the more compact of the older eastern cities; they do not sprawl out forever, although NYC is huge. It is the compactness where I feel in touch with those who live there. I like the differences the City brings, both in terms of ethnicity and in terms of attractions such as shopping and restaurants. All this is very exciting to me. I wouldn't come to the City if it were not exciting.

*   *   *

Continous Thinking: Two Poles With Lots of Space in Between to Rate People

What is stressful for one person is exciting to another. Dr. D. and Kelly just presented a book preview in Denver. Dr. D. couldn't wait to get back to his small Colorado city, while Kelly drove separately so she could stay overnight, soak up the city culture, and experience some excitement. Kelly's comment upon taking the phone call inviting them was: "Great, the winter is long here and The Complex is getting boring. I am ready for a change of venue, and excitement is needed. Surely I can find it in a location in Denver where I have never been."

Michael Apter applies continous logic in his book, **The Dangerous Edge. (Apter 2004)** as it relates to excitement. His continuum, with risk seekers on one end and risk avoiders on the other pole, and everyone somewhere in between, looks like this:

Risk Seekers . . . . Risk Avoiders

This diagram shows the use of continous logic to examine our human behaviors. On the Risk Seekers end, he states: "Risky business activities have never been more popular. Mountain Climbing is America's fastest growing sport as are skiing, mountain biking, river running, ice climbing, and bungee jumping."

On the other end—Risk Avoiders—are people who never do anything where they are not in total control. For example, if they travel, it is with another couple who will adapt to them or they go by themselves. In the journey of life, one doesn't stay in one position on the continiuum. Dr. D., during his twenties to his fifties, was known for the risks he would take in having fun with friends, colleagues, and his family. However, somewhere in his fifth decade, he slid to the left and now is quite cautious. He wouldn't go white-water rafting this summer, has given up skiing even though his seventy-year—old friend is still skiing, takes trips with Nana that he plans but when faced with leaving, doesn't want to go. Yet when they do travel, he enjoys it immensely He is more content to hang onto a rail in a National Park than go a bit out of bounds to see that special site. What used to be pleasure for him has moved more to a negative and is something that arouses anxiety.

It is well known that humans have a stimulation and excitement quota as well as a range in which we will tolerate being a participant. We fill our quotas daily, either positively or negatively, knowingly or unknowlingly, acording to our individual needs. Those that have a high quota and seek to meet it in the public are called extroverts. What most people do not realize is that many introverted indiviudals have a high excitement quota and meet it by doing exciting events alone.

Need for Excitement (or Closure) Leads
Many Brilliant Criminals to Jail

Many bright, resourceful persons carry out detailed crimes and could easily get away with them. However, they get caught, to the amazement of all. Experienced police know that committing the perfect crime is not much fun, because who would know of your accomplishment? As breaking the law and being caught are important to many, our corectional system is full of people who are not valueless criminals who have no guilt, remorse, and can not be rehabilitated. They are just the opposite. When caught, they serve their time and again become law-abiding citizens.[26] Movies sometimes will have two sets of bad guys, one, "the good, bad guys" and the other, "the bad, bad guys." The three-movie

---

[26]   Berne, quoted earlier, sees breaking the law and getting caught, or getting almost caught, as a psychological 'game". He asks, 'what fun is it to do something you know is wrong, bad, or illegal, but to have no one know about it?' Research has shown that many very bright law breakers, like some professional crooks, could go for years committing their crimes that are exciting in their own right without being caught. What then prompts them to be caught suddenly when they could have gotten away with their criminal act again? Many say the excitement, negative as it is, of getting caught, tried, and punished is more important than getting away with the crime.

set of ***Oceans Eleven (1960 & 2001); Oceans Twelve (2004);***[27] ***and Ocean Thirteen***[29] ***(2007)*** are those movie types. An all-time favorite movie is **The Sting** where good, bad guys decide to get even with the Mafia, but have to do so in a way that they are successful without the Mafia ever knowing that they have been had. They do just that!

There it is again, that concept of "excitement." As we learned earlier, there are different types of excitement and excitement needs. Our Forever Family members are enjoying themselves in the summer time. If what we have shared so far, excitement will be a common element and experienced differently as different people have different excitement needs.

*   *   *

At the Beach

At first glance, there is no one anywhere around. Then two heads come up from underneath the water. Nana is first to catch her breath. "I'm so glad that we are vacationing at Hilton Head Island. We are almost up to our necks, and there aren't any big waves to scare me. I can just stand here enjoying myself."

Glancing around and stopping as he turns back towards the beach, Dr. D exclaims: "And the air is so clean and clear and you can see a long way, way up on the beach, to the tree line . . . Hmmm. I am just noticing something, Nana; look at the beach in front of us and the beautiful beach umbrellas, dozens of them. Do you notice how

---

[27]   Already considered a classic www.oceanstwelve.com. See a great trailer at Youtube.com/watch?v=L-EyG12LxME

[28]   Why did they quit with Oceans Thirteen? All drew good crowds; I wanted many more!

so many of them are all packed together in one place, even though there is a lot of beach to spread out on?"

Nana: "You are right, I hadn't really noticed that. I wonder what is going on that draws them together. I know that if my beach umbrella were down there that is just where I would want to be. Right there in the middle where all the action and excitement is!"

One can almost predict Dr. D's answer from the negative look on his face. "Not me, I would be quite a way down the beach where there is some space between me and the other persons. I think there is an interesting contrast going on. So many people were all concerned about having their own space under their umbrella and at the same time were close enough to the other people next to them that they could and often did accidentally touch them? What makes it that way?"

*   *   *

The Big Game in the Big Stadium

The lunch line at the Cave's Deli isn't too long and Dr. D. and Nana are standing in it chatting. He speaks first. "What time do you think Kelly will get here? She has to stop in Atlanta to pick up Vincent at the big game. I wonder if he had a good time. I don't think he had very good seats as that is all his cousin could afford. Oh, here they are now." He waves them to come and get in line with them and since everyone knows they are family, none of the line-dwellers complains.

Vincent: "Hi Nana and Grandpa Dude. I had a great time, a really good time. It was my first time in a stadium that big with so many people. I saw on the big screen that attendance was over 80,000. We didn't have good seats and I could only see the field and the players through our binoculars but that was OK. It was just plain exciting to be there. Boy, were we packed in."

They reached the Deli counter, ordered, and got one of the light and buzzer gizmos that tell you when your order is ready and they go off chatting. Again, it is up to us to figure out the attraction of being crowded into a seat that you paid a lot of money for yet cannot really see the game. I think it is the same as before. The closeness brings contact, even if all are strangers. The contact is exciting as are many other things about a big game. People crave excitement.

*   *   *

Recreational Vehicles (RV's) in an Open Field

Nana is in The Forever Family Complex, in the conference room, waiting for the others to assemble for their staff meeting. She answers the phone and talks quickly to the person calling. She is heard saying: "You're welcome; we're glad we could help. I am glad you are doing well in your anger classes. Uncle Charlie, I have to ask you, where are you? There is a lot of noise in the background. Oh, at the Fairgrounds in an open field. You took your RV there for the week to get a place for the weekend. What are you doing since the state fair doesn't start for four days? . . . I see, just enjoying the camping out, being away from home and away from everybody. But Uncle Charlie, you are hardly away from everybody. I have been out there at fair time and see where your RV is parked and you are packed in there like sardines in a can. What makes that fun? . . . OK, you meant away from anyone who would make you mad. But wouldn't it bother you to be so close to strangers?" To herself, under her breath, she muttered: "I couldn't stay like that. I need my space. Yet he said it is interesting, an exciting location to people watch." She sits back down to wait.

There is that word "excitement" again. It comes up a lot of places where people gather. Perhaps that is one of the reasons we humans gather together so often?

*   *   *

Does Judy Bearister "Kiss and Tell" Or, Again, Just "Kiss?"

Judy, to Dr. D. and Kelly: "I finally told John at lunch about my gambling so I might as well tell you. As you know, I had a gambling problem. I was flying out to visit my mother about once every two months and got a connecting flight through Las Vegas. For some reason, I suddenly did what I have never done before. I had three quarters and went to a slot machine where I quickly lost the first two. So, I stuck that last quarter into the slot machine . . . Oh, My. What a racket! 2500 Pieces of Eight came tumbling out; lights flashed, bells rang, everybody looked and attendants came running. I thought I had done something wrong but I had done something right!

"They had me sign the IRS declaration papers, and then I rushed to the airplane gate and sat in my seat with my check for $32,000 and a cup of coffee, not really knowing what had happened. It was then that the guilt for how I got it really appeared. I could feel mother shaking her finger.

"I got to my Mom's house somehow, never saying a word to her about any of this. We had a pleasant weekend and I forgot the check. However, when I went to put my keys away at home, there it was a check for $32,000 ill-gotten dollars, and a ton of guilt. What do I do about both? The check expires in two days. John wasn't upset at all, especially when he actually saw the check. I feel so guilty; I know what my mother will say. What am I going to do about her?"

Kelly quickly took over. "Judy, guilt isn't a feeling. It is the result of a judgment we have made about something we have done that we think is wrong, something that violates your personal or family values. You think you did badly by sticking those quarters in a slot machine. I bet you wished in one way that you hadn't won as you wouldn't have all this guilt. But you know values, like a feeling, will come up again and again until you do something about it . . . My saying that to you won't matter though, but your mother saying that or something similar will."

Kelly continues. "Here is what you must do as you have no more time. John will be on the phone with you when you call your mother. After your greetings, I want you to say: 'Mom, I have some exciting news to share . . .' Then share a summary of how you got the money. Then, ask her what she thinks. John will have called her about an hour before to explain the situation and what you want to do with the money. I think she will tell you what you want to hear and that old guilt, that rascal, will disappear for a while. Then, as you are cashing that check, call and see if we can spend fifteen minutes together chasing away the rest of that rascal."

Judy: "I like that. John told me that you two would help. Thank you so much, both of you." Judy then left to go home.

Dr. D. and Kelly just looked at each other for a while and then Dr. D. smiled. "What a woman. It made my day how you helped her. Time is flying by and I have to go to The Complex's control room to record my summary. Can you come now or will you do yours later?"

Kelly: "Now is best. I need some caffeine. Meet you in the control room in ten."

Dr. D.'s Famous Summary Ending.

Dr. D: "The key to life is the making of human contact, which if done in the right way, can lead to excitement. Excitement is short lived and must be repeatedly obtained. It is like having a snowball outside on the 4th of July. Excitement is a human need sought through our families, inanimate objects, and people in our lives that are important to us. As with other relationships, the payoffs may be good for us or not. Offered were some steps one can take to manage our feelings and our excitement. But then again, there are always things to learn!"

© Dr. D.'s Domains 2013`

Chapter Twelve

Grandma Knows.

Author: Nancy Cogswell, R.N.

*At the end of your life you will never regret not having passed
one more test, not winning one more verdict,
or not closing one more deal.
You will regret time not spent with a husband,
a friend, a child or a parent."*

Barbara Bush, Reflections: Life after the White House

Grandmas are Moms with lots of frosting.

Author Unknown

Nana Listens to Vincent

A few miles away from the Forever Family Complex, Nana is busy in her condo. She decided to work from home today as she wanted a day without people. Then the telephone rang.

"Hello, Vincent. How did you hear that I was at home all of today? . . . Oh, well, our office manager Jane told you and she knows you are my grandson . . . Yes, of course I would like a visit from you. Can you come at lunch time and we will have lunch and some chocolate chip cookies I'm baking. Good, you know where to park your bike and I will see you around noon."

She hung up and went back to her reading thinking: "If it were not that Vincent is my so loveable fifteen-year-old grandson, I would have said no. I wonder what is on his mind."

A while later, at noon, Nana heard a bike's brakes squeal and saw Vincent out her den window. He knocked and without waiting for an answer bounded into the kitchen where he greeted her. She was glad that even at age fifteen, he would still hug her. She loved that part of their relationship. She hoped it would continue to be a part of their greeting.

One could tell by Vincent's smile that he was glad to be here and Nana wondered if it were more than the cookies. Vincent began. "I've been thinking about your chocolate chip cookies all morning. You know how I like them—thanks for making them for me."

Nana: "So what brings you out here today?"

With no hesitation, Vincent began to share. "I just wanted to chat about something that happened at school . . . I came across a group of girls that I know talking in the hall. I overheard some of their conversation but didn't stay to join in. What I heard surprised me and I didn't know what to think. I didn't want to ask either."

Nana encouraged him to continue. "So what did you hear, Vincent?"

"I heard one of the girls say that 'Sally really did it!' All the girls seemed very surprised. Since I didn't know what to make of that, I asked another friend, a boy who also knows Sally. He said he wondered if that meant she had hooked up with her new boyfriend. We both had questions about that and wondered if that could possibly be true. It was unsettling to both of us because we thought she wasn't the type of girl who would get this involved with a new boyfriend.

"My friend told someone else that Sally had hooked up with her new boyfriend and that information spread around pretty quickly. As it turned out, that was totally untrue but wasn't set straight until several people were upset. It seems that what the girls were talking about was that Sally had turned in her application to become a cheerleader for football season, something she said she would never do. She had always said she was afraid of being injured with the gymnastic part and those pyramids. I am feeling responsible for this misinformation, as I was the person who started the story."

Nana responded with a great deal of warmth in her voice. "Friendship is complicated Vincent, and it takes work to keep our valued friendships strong. You have just seen how a mishearing, followed by a misspeaking can affect a relationship. Continue to be her friend. Remember to find out the truth before you speak to another. This is a lesson that will be learned many times in your life." Vincent smiled and spoke. "Thanks, Nana. I am feeling better about this now and will remember what you told me. I'm so glad I have you to talk to about some of these things."

"I am too, Vincent," Nana says with a smile and a gentle hug." Now let's have some cookies."

Learning is Also Forever

Chocolate chip cookies weren't the focus of this dialog, but they do help soothe the soul. What we read was a conversation between a grandma and her grandson who trusted her enough to share what was on his mind. Nana was able to comfort Vincent and learn a life lesson that may need to be repeated again in the future. M. Scott Peck, world-renowned psychiatrist and author, offers this about the meaning of life: "I believe the reason we are here is to learn, which is to say we evolve or to progress. When people learn, they are in a position to pro-gress (move forward) as opposed to re-gress (move backward). And I defy you in your imagination to construct a more ideal environment for human learning than this life." (Peck, 1997, p. 95).

*　*　*

Teaching is Out and Mentoring is In

Dr. D. has arrived at his condo that he shares with his wife, Nana. With several chocolate chip cookies in hand, he offers his thoughts on learning in extended families. "Once away from school, people generally do not think they need to be taught something. However, they will respond positively to the concept of mentoring. Wikipedia offers as good an explanation of mentoring as I have ever read."

> Mentorship is different than teaching overall but has many common elements. It is the process where a more experienced or more knowledgeable person helps to guide a less experienced or less knowledgeable person. However, true mentoring is more than just answering occasional questions or providing ad hoc help. It is about an ongoing relationship of learning, dialog, and challenge. (Unknown, 2013).

Nana accepts that information and takes one of the chocolate cookies back from her husband's hand for herself. She then adds: "This is one of the privileges we have of being a grandparent, sharing what we know about life. Our mentoring function starts with some general rules:

- Information is worthless without experience (Dr. Albert Einstein);

- Share what you know as sharing is free, both to you who shares and the person who receives your gift;

- Doing something about what is shared is the second step. That is why it is up to the listener, your adult son or daughter, granddaughter, or grandson, to decide whether to follow the suggestion."

*   *   *

157

Our Turn is Now

Parent and Ende, in their book, *How to Raise Your Adult Children*, start off their chapter on Grandchildren with these thoughts:

> Grandchildren are a treat for us grandparents. Unlike their own parents, we have the time and space to observe and reflect on their growth and development. We don't have to buy diapers and we can buy a cute little party dress, which is more fun. We are not on the firing line, having to make myriad decisions each day the way our kids do. When we're tired, the grandkids go home. We put our houses back in order and keep them that way until the much-loved grandchildren come for another visit. It's perfect, isn't it? Well, not exactly. When we were growing up, grandparents were often part of the child-rearing team. They were consulted and involved. They were respected for their wisdom (Parent, 2010, p. 216)

The Importance of Extended and Intergenerational Family Activities

Grandparents are different from one another in relation to age, race, culture, and ideologies and more. One thing we share is that we are the heart of the extended family. Along with aunts, uncles, cousins, and others, we are the older ones in the family who have lived the history and can share that with younger family members. We are the foundation that exists for all of our families' beliefs and values. "There is no foundation, no secure ground, upon which people may stand today if it isn't the family . . . If you don't have the support, love, caring and concern that you get from family, you don't have much at all. Love is so supremely important . . . This is the part of what a family is about, not just love, but letting others know there's someone who is watching out for them. It's what I call your spiritual security." (Albom, 1997, p. 91).

Covey in his book, **The 7 Habits of Highly Effective Families**, speaks especially to how the grandparents have become involved through the taking of normal activities—family times and Sunday dinners—and expanded them to include members of their extended and intergenerational families. "Extended and intergenerational family members can be involved in almost everything you do. Over the years, Sandra and I have made it a point to go to our children's programs, recitals, and sporting events or whatever individual family members were involved in. We've tried to provide a support system to the family members to show that we care and that each person in the family is appreciated and loved. We always have an open invitation for anyone in the extended and intergenerational family who can come to such activities. And Sandra and I often attend the activities that involve our brothers and sisters and their families as well." (Covey, 1997, p. 296).

Covey's extended families lived in close geographic proximity to each other so daily or weekly involvement was possible. We offer some guidelines for parenting that includes some ideas about relating when you live at a distance.

Some Guidelines for Grand Parenting

- What do you call yourself in this new role? Discuss preferences and compromise to get to a name used by all your grandchildren. If your own adult children support that name, the grandkids will use it as well. This establishes your importance as a family member;

- Be creative in the use of these electronic devices. Kisses, cookies, hugs, and the latest school project can be shared/ given via the electronic device on both ends, and they will be received and sent as eagerly as if you were in the room.[29] Remember the long ago (1964) Bell Telephone Company's famous slogan when the telephone was made popular: "It is the next best thing to being there!"[30] If the parents will permit it, a treat for both can be a short call to you to share something e.g. to inquire about how you are doing in recovering from your cold or your flu, just like you did when they were sick;

- When you travel, postcards and pictures in letters sent directly to your grandchildren are always welcomed;

- These sweet grandchildren are not yours. They belong to your children;

- Support the parents' authority even when you might not agree with them;

- It is very important that the child sees that we as their grandparents will enforce the same rules as their parents. Children learn very quickly how to play the game "Divide and Conquer" when the parents and grandparents are divided on the rules of behavior;

---

[29] Our eighteen month-old granddaughter often asks to talk on the phone with Nana and Papa. We wonder if, when we are not visiting her, she thinks we live in the phone. After all, we know of other young adults of our kid's generation, now parents, who used to think that their Grandmother lived at the local airport as that is where they went to get her when Grandma flew to see them.

[30] If you want to relive a bit of history, go to http://www.classicrotaryphones. com/advertisements4.html and see some of the ads for telephone usage that we all were hooked by. They were really well done and did us as Americans ever respond to them.

- Your role is to be a nonjudgmental, loving grandparent. Children thrive on being valued and this is where our role is so important. We are there as the frosting on the cake.

Staying Healthy With Your Grandchildren

Staying healthy does have its challenges. Practicing some simple strategies helps keep everyone healthy. Immunizations are important for grandparents, parents, and grandchildren alike. All need to have flu shots every year, particularly if the grandparents are over sixty-five and the children are at least six months old. The older person, as well as the very young, is the most at risk for the flu and its complications. If grandparents spend much time with the children, it becomes even more important. Grandparents also need to be up to date with the TDAP (Tetanus, Diphtheria, and Pertussis) vaccination. This is a change to the regular every ten-year Tetanus shot. It has been shown that the youngest children, from birth to about one year, do not have adequate immunity to pertussis (whooping cough) as their shot series has not been completed. Recently, there have been an increased number of cases of pertussis in our country among infants that experts at the Centers for Disease Control and Prevention (CDC)[31] feel may be originating with undiagnosed infections in adults. These adults have close contact with these young babies and thus the infection is passed on.[32] This can be a significant disease for a young baby and may even be fatal. This simple action of getting this vaccination can save a life.

Hand washing cannot be over emphasized thus it is always recommended to do frequent hand washing when around young

---

[31] For more information, go to www.cdc.gov/immunizations

[32] It has been forgotten how serious the disease pertussis still is as it has almost been eliminated by the regular vaccination of children. Yet it still exists and still surfaces occasionally in this country.

children to prevent the spread of colds, flu, gastro—intestinal disruptions as well as other common infections. As grandparents, we may not be around our grandkids often enough to build immunities to their germs, so we are susceptible, as are they to our germs. It is not surprising that after an extended visit with the children, the grandparent(s) will often come down with whatever was going around. This is exactly what happened after one of our recent visits; it took us two weeks to get over what we caught from them.

Enjoy the Journey. Receive by Giving

Dr. D. is now in the room and he begins to share. "Conflict is a part of all families' lives, even among grandparents and grandchildren who have a great relationship. I had a grandmother call me up this week to ask about what she could do about a relationship/ communication in this situation. Her son and his wife have two kids, ages five and three. The two grandparents and their offspring with the children like to go out to eat about once a week. However, the two kids go wild when in the restaurant, dumping the sugar out of the restaurant's sugar packets, combining the contents of the salt and pepper shakers, playing hide and seek under tablecloths of unoccupied tables, speaking in loud voices, and generally running wild. The father's response is ineffective in controlling his kids; he keeps urging the waiter to bring the kids' food so that they will be distracted. The mother ignores their behavior by talking to her friends on her cell phone. Both parents' passive responses signal the children that what they are doing is OK.

"The Grandparents recognize that there is no discipline, but when they tell that to their son, they are told, 'This really isn't any of your concern, these are our kids.' The grandparents know better and want to know what to do."

Nana has also returned. "This is a common occurrence and I have had many grandparents in my clinics talk to me about the same thing. What I tell them first is how normal a problem this is and how important it is that they are willing to do something about it. What I suggest is a three-step process. The first step is to come prepared with some items to entertain the kids while they wait for dinner. Grandma's purse can be a wonderful place for kids this age, as can be Grandpa's pockets. The second step is to say nothing either to the kids or the parents as to what is wrong[33] but instead to address the kids on what is wanted. Say something like this: 'Susan and Johnny, come over here to Grandma while we wait for our food. I have some things in my purse that I think you will like.' Grandpa can help by also having some things in his pockets that will interest them. Grandma will usually know what to bring in her purse from experience. Kid's card games, markers and crayons, Legos, books, and games on the cell phone are good. Do not let the kids take the games and plays by themselves but maintain control over the games and the grandkids at all times. Share the fun of playing with them, which will help keep them under control while you wait. You are in effect teaching your grandchildren and your son and wife restaurant manners and mentoring the two other adults in how to discipline."

Dr. D. offers more: "The third step is to provide and reinforce any additional structure that seems natural to the family. If the family is one that prays before a meal, say a short prayer with everyone and then eat. The structure says to the kids there is order to life, even when away from home. All people seek structure at all ages. Even the chaos of the playtime described above is structure, undesirable

---

[33] Even though you think you are speaking to what is wrong and are not on the case of either, you will be perceived as being judgmental and putting them down. Instead of reinforcing what you don't want, speak to what is wanted and reinforce that.

as it may be to the grandparents. Help the parent learn how to parent in a specific situation."

Kelly is very eager to share. "I have an example to which parents with younger kids can relate. I am the coach of 'The Comets,' an under-14 girls' soccer team. I use the same principles and recipes that I use in counseling with these girls. I never, never yell anything negative at them. I always talk with them about what I want, never what I don't want.

"Here is an example. We are in a close game and the other team has a very fast forward, No. 14. She is apt to score at any time and I want to make sure she doesn't get the ball and beat us all on her own. I take out briefly my defender on that side, who is daydreaming a bit and not guarding No.14 the way I want her to do. I say: 'Jamie, I want No.14 to be kept away from even touching the ball. That means you have to stay very, very close to her every second when their team has control of the ball. Touch her shirt as often as you can but not enough to catch the attention of the referee. Run with her. When she stops, you stop.'

"When we have the ball, move away and do your thing offensively, But when they have the ball, get very close to No. 14 . . . Jamie, tell me what you have heard me say so I know you understand . . . That is good; No 14 is in trouble with you guarding her. Now get a drink, rest a bit and in a couple of minutes, I will put you back in the game. I want to get Susan some playing time also as No. 14 can really wear out one defender."

"The girls really respond well to this approach. If Jamey doesn't get it or can't stay with No.14, I take her off the field again, and repeat what I said and did before, then put her right back in. No yelling about mistakes, only positive statements and mentoring about what I want. I make sure my other coaches do the same. Remember, like a grandparent or parent, a major portion of our coaching role is to teach or mentor. The parents will figure out our style, love you for it, and reinforce it at home. It is a win-win all the way . . . By the way, we are undefeated so far."

Dr. D. cups his hands around his mouth and yells, "Way to go Kelly and the Comets." Kelly is so excited by Dr. D.'s excitement; she dribbles her ball two steps and kicks it solidly out the door. She shrugs and says to no one in particular. "Well, that wasn't very smart. Now I have to go and find it as we need that for tomorrow's practice."

Nana came in the door just as the ball was exiting. She ducked it calmly, thinking to herself: "This is just like at home when Vincent and Lucy kick the ball back and forth from the living room to the porch, going through the kitchen. I just dodge and keep on going."

"Learn to enjoy applesauce, a product from an apple that falls from a tree but does not roll away. Learn to support your AC's being the one to make the applesauce and to adopt his/her recipe."

Dr. D.: "I have always liked applesauce and apple butter in the fall and apple strudel and apples in pancakes and especially a Dutch apple pie . . . Whoa, that all make me hungry . . . but then again, Kelly did make an Apple Crumb Cake and I have some of it for us to taste. Let's stop working for now and go eat some of it!"

Nana: "I'll get the plates and forks. You do the summary that we always do."

Dr. D.'s Famous Summary

Dr. D. "In closing, remember most all apples fall from the tree, and may have some bruises, but they are still just bruises and good apples. Enjoy them and the challenges of making good dishes with them. Remember all our children and grandchildren are different from each other even though they may come from the same tree. As always, feelings will be there, but by now, you know about feelings and what to do with them. Awareness of feelings is nothing more than 'awareness of feelings.' However, doing something about them is what is important. We've given you tools to use and an understanding of what to do with them in relation to your family. Remember, there is always more to learn."

© Dr. D.'s Domains 2013

Chapter Thirteen
Truisms for Parents

I didn't fail the test. I just found 100 ways to do it wrong.

Benjamin Franklin

If I agreed with you, we'd both be wrong.

We never really grow up; we only learn how to act in public.

Winston Churchill

From Wild West Virginia to the Wild West

Banjo music deep inside a mountain? Both Dr. D. and Hobs, one of our guest bakers and Forever Family philosopher, heard it. But from where? There was no radio or stereo on, none of the rooms had windows. It must be coming from the hall but no one at The Complex played the banjo. The music sounded like one part of Dr. D's favorite banjo music, *Dueling Banjos*, and as he was thinking about that piece, who came strumming in but a longtime friend of his, Dr. Everett Lilly. "Hi, folks," Everett exclaimed. "I had real trouble locating you all . . . but I did. Quite a complex you have here. I have never played music in a cave before. I wonder how the acoustics would be way down here. Well, now I know. When I was playing in the hall, my banjo sounded really great."

Dr. D. introduced Everett to Hobs, and asked "What brings you from West to West?"

Everett smiled and strummed a cord. "Our family's Bluegrass band, The Sound Catchers, is playing at Red Rocks amphitheater in Denver tomorrow and we practice late this afternoon. When we arrived, I realized where you were doing your writing so asked around, got directions, and here I am. I do have a question now that I look around your office and see all the signs with quotes. How can I get some of those for our practice facilities in Beckley, West Virginia? I sure do enjoy them whenever I see them."

Nana and Kelly had also heard the banjo music and were equally puzzled. They too followed the strumming and appeared in the office as well. More introductions were given, Everett's question re-asked, and Kelly handed Everett a folder with a manuscript in it. "We were just working on those truisms this morning with Hobs. Here is our latest version of the last chapter of Book One. Take it with you; I'll print out another copy later."

Everett thanked her, surprised along with everyone else at the quickness of the reply. Kelly then said: "I'll take you for a tour of this place if you will test out the acoustics along the way by playing some more for us." Everett agreed and off Kelly, Everett, Hobs, Nana and Dr. D. went to listen to good Bluegrass and show off The Complex. Nana thought to herself: "I am glad Dr. D. got to see his Everett, but I sure hope my husband doesn't try to sing along."

* * *

The American Extended Family

I was on the way to Dr. D.'s office for that writing meeting when this musical troupe went by me. Dr. D. yelled: "You know the script. Carry on without us." So I will.

Truisms are short sayings that explain something or contain advice to our 21st century American family. People who work with families often call the family that one grows up in, the nuclear family, and the family that one forms after one leaves home, an extended family. Using these terms is easy; nothing else about these two types of families is easy or uncomplicated. For example, the idea of a nuclear family seems straight forward until one begins to realize that the example we begin with of a mom, dad, and some number of kids has changed over the last decade to include:

- Blended families, which are those families where mom and/ or dad have remarried and reconstituted another nuclear family; Single parent families where, because of divorce or separation, either mom or dad is left to raise the children;

- Increasingly among Generation X, Y or Z'ers, gay/ lesbian families where two people of the same gender cohabitate and raise the children of previous unions from roles representative of mother and female roles; separated/ divorced nuclear families where mom and dad become divorced or separated, and one or both remarry or move in with someone;

- This creates a multiple layer set of nuclear families. Regardless of the form, when emerging adults marry, as they are increasingly doing so later on in their twenties,[34] or move in with a serious relationship partner, they form an extended family.

The extended family in its basic form is made up of the original mom and dad (or new combination), any children still living at home, the adult child that has moved out into their own nuclear family, their spouse, and any children they have now produced. In numbers, it is a much bigger version of the nuclear family. In function, it is similar to the original nuclear family in that it has its own values, norms, boundaries, roles, and rules that build on with what the new heads of the family grew up believing. It also

---

[34] The average age of marriage for an emerging female has moved from twenty-two to twenty-eight.

introduces and/or combines new values, norms, boundaries, roles, and rules to which they contribute and adapt. The amount of difference in each extended family from their nuclear family may or may not vary tremendously. As each grown-up child becomes a head of their own nuclear family, they are actually also in two extended families. One is related to their own parents and one is related to the parents of their spouse. Thus when it is all added up, an adult child goes from primarily being a member of one family, their original nuclear family, to being a member of three families. It is no wonder things get confused for all and conflicts become much more pronounced.

People have been studying families from decades from all kinds of perspectives including religious approaches, family dynamics approaches and even business models and philosophy approaches. Because we are counselors, we are going to use one of eight popular family dynamics approaches, but it doesn't really differ much from the approach Jesus would take or a team builder in a Fortune 500 business.[35]

Characteristics of Successful Extended Families

Our families of focus are extended families, those families that include several generations of members. Successful extended families throughout the generations have a combination of dimensions that include:

(1) A structure to it that is well-known by all members, has stood the test of time, and has a realistic leadership system in place. In our extended family, that typically includes three generations of family members, starting with the

---

[35] Becvar & Becvar, 1999, **Systems theory and family therapy. A primer**. Washington, D.C. University Press of America, p. 103.

grandparents, known as the patriarch and matriarch, or First Father and Mother. The second generation in this hierarchical are the parents of the children/grandchildren of this extended family. Both sets of parents lead, in different ways, and at different levels of the family structure;

(2) An established rule system that basically focuses on the communication patterns of everyone and on the behaviors that members are allowed to exhibit while in the presence of the Extended Family. An example would be either the permission to swear or the prohibition against doing so;

(3) All family members, starting with the smallest members, are clearly cared for and loved in as many active ways as possible. It is clear that this carries forth to the First Father and Mother, who are often by our broad cultural standards, shuttled off to institutions such as nursing homes;

(4) Effective ways of caring for the babies up through the launching time, usually after high school graduation, are in place and supported by all the adults;

(5) A respect for the institution of marriage and supports put in place for those married couples in the Extended Family;

(6) A set of goals toward which the family and each individual works, and;

(7) Sufficient flexibility by everyone, starting with the First Father and Mother and moving downward that results in the adaptability to accommodate normal developmental challenges as well as unexpected crises.

* * *

Truisms Explained

Having given Everett the tour and listened to his music, Kelly, Dr. D., Nana, and Hobs came back to the office to discuss and write about the truisms on which they were focusing. Kelly began the conversation: "Let us look at how different truisms, short sayings that explain something or contain advice, relate to and support our Forever Extended Family recipe. The first Truism is: ***Too many cooks spoil the stew!*** This is an old saying that means if you have too many leaders, things don't go well. How does this relate to parenting our adult offspring?"

Dr. D., still humming a favorite tune, explained: "For Parents of Emerging Adults (EA) (18-29) or Young Adults (YA) (30-40), this is an issue that has been with them the whole time they have been a parent. Remember when you were teaching your youngster how to tie his/her shoes and (s) he had to do it his/her way? Even in adulthood, this is often a major issue as to who is going to be in charge or command. The drive for independence is a VERY strong one. It can overpower logic or even family tradition. Parents of grown children need to know this is happening and that it is normal. They will benefit from being aware that their feelings related to loss of control are very natural and common. That will help a little bit with the change.

"Parents of emerging/young adults have to step back and let their off-spring be in control, even if you know better on an issue, or can do something better. Being right isn't the most important thing here. Your Adult Child wants to experience the thrill and joy of being the leader, of being in control. (S)he values learning more by her/his own experience than by learning from the experience of those who have already thought it out or 'been there, done that.' Parents have to step back and give up that position, not always, but often! Remember, you didn't want your parents to always tell you what to do."

Kelly: "As a mid-thirties-some Young Adult, I experienced battles with my parents over that issue. It wasn't that I didn't value their knowledge and experience, I just wanted to do it myself."

Hobs knew it was his turn to explain. He picked a truism that he knew well: "Another Truism is *A son is a son until he takes a wife; a daughter is a daughter all her life*. This relates to the attachment that many sons have to their spouse in place of their previous relationship with their parents. It is in contrast to what a daughter does when she gets married; she adds the relationship with her new spouse to that to her parents and work to maintain both. Both a son and a daughter are members of the Extended Family; this Truism speaks to the tendency each has to relate strongly or not so strongly to their original parents. This leadership just doesn't happen for those parties that they go to; it typically extends in many other ways. If before marriage the two engaged persons belong to different religions, it is typically the male who will change to his new wife's religion. When kids come into the family, it is most often the parents of their children's kids to whom they relate. However, when there is a choice, it is typical for one mom to talk to another mom and end up arranging something for the two families to do. Hopefully your married children will take a 'blended family' approach with norms and ways of doing things borrowed from both sides of the family. Again, if a couple is going to be closer to one set of parents, it is likely to be the female's parents. Finally, when a baby is due, even if your daughter-in-law has a solid and active relationship with you, she is still most likely to want to have her mother be there at the actual time of birth."

Kelly has warmed her coffee and picks up the sharing: "Our third Truism for this month is: *"Having an Emerging or Young Adult means a change in roles for both parties. It is hard for Parents to have their children reach adulthood and adjust to their own renewed autonomy and separateness, let alone experience the loss of control or being in lead role and other changes that come along naturally."*

"What is typically focused upon is the need for the parents to change. Often overlooked are changes for the adult offspring make in their relationship with their parents. They don't stop having parents but have to learn how to relate in different ways. One change for the adult offspring is to accept that their new independence comes with new responsibilities to give back. Our kids know about being the center of attention and given to by their parents. When they reach adult status, if their Parents are to adjust, they also need to adjust. Friends, colleagues, and others who become more important to the semi-liberated parent won't meet all their needs. Adult children can give back by being good listeners, asking about activities, jobs/retirement, and other events in their parents' lives. Too many continue to get but don't give back."

"Parents, this is not a natural transition so you may have to ask for and mentor your EY/YA on giving back in ways other than having grandchildren. Learn to ask them for what you want."

Hobs, who for years taught college courses on the family, picks three from that background: "I've got three related Truisms: *(A). Families Very Actively Resist Change; (B). Families Change all the Time."* These beliefs actually go together and do not contradict each other. Change is resisted actively by all organisms, although eventually occurring. e.g. families tend to want graduating high school seniors to stay at home but eventually send them off to college, the beginning of this change. Families do not easily go from nuclear to extended families, but they do. Parents do not easily become empty nesters, but they do typically become empty nesters."

(C) "Not only do families change, but what we know about family dynamics continues to change. From the 1960s to the 1990s people and counselors specifically believed all problems that existed with children in a family were mostly to be blamed on poor parenting. That is no longer the case. A good counselor, when presented an issue, looks to see what multiple factors have come into play to produce the negative or unwanted results. They then focus on behavior and what can be changed now and in the future. There is little history taking as we know much more about human behavior and relationships than we did fifty years ago. So, if your Emerging/Young Adult wants to blame his parents, don't accept that and look elsewhere."

*   *   *

Human Change is like Changing Keys in Music, Important and Difficult

Kelly: "Is change easy?"

Dr. D.: "No way! And I believe that the older one gets, the harder it is to change, although I don't have any research to back that up."

Kelly: "I'll comment on the two related truisms just mentioned: (A) *All People Resist Change* and (B) *Change is Inevitable.*

"These seem to contradict each other but they both are correct. The first one is: 'All people resist change' We like things to go well and humans seek out homeostasis or a standing still condition. As 'homeostasis' came from biology, a medical definition is appropriate. We like to be healthy. Our bodies try to maintain our health but eventually break down. Wikipedia, the free encyclopedia, states this: "Every illness has aspects to it that are a result of lost homeostasis. Just as we live in a constantly changing world, so do the cells and tissues survive in a constantly changing microenvironment. The 'normal' or 'physiologic' state then is achieved by adaptive responses to the ebb and flow of various stimuli permitting the cells and tissues to adapt and to live in harmony within their microenvironment. Thus, homeostasis is preserved. It is only when the stimuli is severe, or the response of the organism breaks down, that disease results—a generalization as true for the whole organism as it is for the individual cell. (Robins, 1984).'

"Author George Leonard, in his 2010 book, *The Keys to Success and Long Term Fulfillment* discusses how homeostasis affects behavior and who we are. He states that homeostasis will prevent our body from making drastic changes and maintaining stability in our lives even if it is detrimental. e.g. when an obese person starts exercising, homeostasis in the body resists the activity to maintain stability; an unstable family where the father has been a raging alcoholic and suddenly stops and the son starts up a drug habit to maintain stability in the family. Homeostasis is the main factor that stops people changing their habits because our bodies view change as dangerous unless it is very slow. Leonard discusses this dilemma as the media today only encourages fast change and quick results. The opening of his book aptly describes his despair with the current state of the world and how it is at war with homeostasis. 'The trouble is that we have few, if any, maps to guide us on the journey or even to show us how to find the path. The modern world, in fact, can be viewed as a prodigious conspiracy against mastery. We're continually bombarded with the promises of immediate gratification, instant success, and fast, temporary relief, all of which lead in exactly the wrong direction.'" (Leonard, 1992).

Thinking about one of the families the Barristers have talked about with us, Dr. D. commented: "This first statement, that all people resist change, is important for all adult family members to comprehend. Just because a client comes to you wanting to change doesn't mean that they will or that it is easy. Don't expect them to accept everything you have to offer or the suggestions that you make. Expect resistance. Know what to do to help people go about changing because they need your help as much in how to go about changing as what to change."

*   *   *

Six Short Takes on Truisms for People Who are Hurrying Through Life

No matter how angry or busy or distant they or you are from each other, never lose contact.

It is human nature to avoid the unpleasant. When one person argues with another, what is called the "fight-flight syndrome" is engaged. If two family members argue, typically one member either fights or flees, leaving the scene or situation. Both actions break contact and the essence of human relationship is making contact.

If you want to get something done, ask a busy person.

One of the givens in western societies is all humans have twenty-four hours each day to live their lives, no more and no less. We have all tried to change that through wishing. "Today is so long, will it never end" or "what a day, I wish it would never end." If we all equally possess the same amount of time each day, then why do some people get more done than others do? A business or corporation often employs time management experts to teach skills to help individuals become effective and efficient by showing each employee how to identify and focus on task activities that provide the greatest returns.

It may be just the opposite of what is claimed.

Some parents of extended families end up hearing the claim: "You just want to control me and everything I do." What actually may be happening is that this is your offspring's way of working to your behavior! When this happens, people come across aggressively as a defense. In this case, hold your ground. Speak to feelings, not the content: "You are very angry right now."

Observe the Forest for the Trees.

With any issue, there is always more than the obvious. When there is an obvious "drama" going on within your Extended Family, pay special attention to the little things about the family and right there you will have the opportunity to observe and comment on what is happening, the roles everyone plays, the emotional tone of everyone, and finally the communication patterns used either to accomplish something or to block other's success. It is the "forest view" that will let you learn from experience and transfer learning from one situation to another.

When Important, Contract to Listen/Discuss.

When jumping right into a subject, the other person's mind is on something else. To get their attention so they will concentrate on what you want, then you should ask: "Could we talk right now about _____?" If they say "Yes," then go into what you want to discuss. If they say "No," ask either (1) "Could we talk after supper?" or (2) "When would be a good time for you to talk about _____?"

Thinking is Thinking, Feeling is Feeling, and Doing is a Step Beyond Both.

When you think, you use information. Feelings involve short emotional reactions to something. One can also think about feelings. Thinking about feeling may use the word "feeling" in the sentence such as: "I don't feel good about that paint color." Doing is a behavior that involves either thinking or feeling first and then an action step. You do something like "throw the ball" or "actually call David on the telephone" or "you drive the car to work." Doing is an advanced brain function and usually has more of a payoff. Doing is necessary for change to occur.

*   *   *

Dr. D.'s Favorite Summary

Dr. D. pauses before he speaks as the moment is important. "All of us in the Forever and Bearister families are feeling both happy and sad that this is the last regular chapter in our book. We hope you have learned much about families and taken some of our recipes to apply to your extended family. In all that occurs always enjoy the journey because you may never get to the destination or, when you do, you will be too old to remember anything along the way. We have offered you our thoughts about what makes things the way that they are. Remember, there is always more to learn. Goodbye and journey well."

As always, Kelly gets the next to last word. "Goodbye to all and I hope to meet up with you in Book Two that deals with those rascals, our feelings"

You the reader get the last word because this book has been all about you and your family. You are always in a family and that doesn't change. As others have stated, "Journey well!"

© 2013 Dr. D.'s Domains

Chapter Fourteen: A Bonus Chapter

Family Money Matters: When & How to Financially Assist Your Offspring.

Guest Author: Sir Roger Bell

Only a life lived for others is a life worthwhile.

Dr. Albert Einstein

Contrast President John Kennedy's mantra of "ask not what you can do for yourself but ask what you can do for your country" with President Ronald Reagan's mantra of "are you better off today than you were four years ago?" What does that tell you about the mess that we do have today?

Auto insurance can be much less expensive if we as a society would focus on replacing or restoring one's damaged property to its original state and on paying for needed medical care instead of making money on accidents. It is well known how to make the change, but no one is listening.

Dr. Dennis Cogswell

The Sage of Aunt Sarah's Mega Cash

The room was full. Of course Dr. D. was there in his comfortable leather chair that he had rescued from Hubert Hummer. In the right corner sat Kelly with her classy mat underneath her classy coffee cup. It was her usual place, where she could see everything. Today, she had a cup with an evergreen tree with a squirrel that climbed up and down the tree as coffee was added to or drunk from the cup. John and Judy Bearister were in the leather chairs to the right of Dr. D. To the left of Kelly sat one of their key guest bakers, Sir Roger Bell, their financial planner and primary author of this chapter. There was one empty chair in the middle with no one scheduled to fill that during this conference.

Dr. D. was pleased. This was a very fine group of people. They would be having a good summary conference. Judy Bearister was about to speak to Kelly about her plans for vacation and then the phone rang . . ."

All looked puzzled, especially Dr. D. His office staff knew they were in conference and would only interrupt them in an emergency. What could be wrong?

He answered the phone and indeed it was his long-time office manager. He listened carefully to her and finally said: "Welcome her and definitely bring her up."

He hung up, looked at the group, and only spoke with his gestures. They were, the palms of his hands up, a wrinkled brow, his head going east to west and back; then he closed his eyes to wait.

Soon the Complex's elevator door opened up. Jane came in, making sure that the woman behind her followed. Jane did so in a way that was gracious towards her as she wasn't sure Dr. D. would be. "Everyone, this is Aunt Sarah from Syracuse. She just got in on the noon bus from Chicago. She rode the Greyhound all the way from Syracuse, stopping in Cleveland, Toledo, Ohio, and some small towns before she got to Chicago and changed buses." Aunt Sarah spoke up for the first time: "Yes, that is exactly 1687 miles, which took us three days total although we were only moving for twenty-six hours plus some minutes. It was long, especially between Davenport, Iowa, and Kearney, Nebraska. It was there that the onboard bathroom didn't work and the driver wouldn't stop long enough for anyone to do their business."

Everyone just looked at this very bright lady who looked like Mary Poppins when she first arrived at the Banks house in London to become their Nanny[36]. Their glance quickly went beyond her to the two grocery food bags she had, one under each arm, along with a satchel. The bags were packed full, and sealed with duct tape. Still, there was a rip in one and something green stuck out. It fluttered to the floor, watched by everyone. Jane, the ever observant office manager, moved first. She picked up the fifty dollar bill and handed it to Sarah, who took it as if she deserved to be waited on.

"Hi Ya, Sonny." Aunt Sarah spoke loudly to Dr. D., not waiting for an introduction. "I am sure glad that you are here as these bones are tired and need to be put up for a while. I aim to get to California to catch me my second hubby. I met Samuel online at the Old Time Family Bingo game which we both played weekly and were often the winners. We met in chat rooms everywhere, and he surprised me by proposing and I surprised him by saying yes. Then we had the problem that I lived one place and he lived another and it is a long way between there and there. But I found that the Hound goes out there and as California doesn't have anywhere near as much snow as Syracuse, we agreed to meet and marry there. I just need to rest a bit before I get back on the Hound for the final leg." She stopped, as if that told it all.

What could anyone say? This road-weary looking lady, who talked fast and yet made a lot of sense and was clearly in charge of her life, was now in charge of the six of them with no effort at all.

---

[36]   This well-known story first opened up as a Disney movie in 1964. Its story line was that a magic nanny comes to work for a cold banker's unhappy family. The Play's first performance was on June 4, 2008 in London. http://en.wikipedia.org/wiki/Mary_Poppins_(musical)

Their looks finally went back to the bags. What were they full of? And if it were what people were thinking, how did she get all of it?

So Sarah spoke again. "Sonny, you got a head here? I am full and better do something about it. I will leave my satchel and these full bags with you as I have always known you to be an honest man and know you will take good care of them. I'll be back in five and we can continue our talk." She left, as if she knew the way around the cave. Soon she was heading down the elevator.

Kelly was closer to the bags than Dr. D., so she reached over and felt one. "It's solid but soft. Feels like wads of paper. Could it all actually be what came out of the top and Jane picked up? She clearly gave Sarah back a hundred dollar bill."

It was here that Dr. D. stood up and whispered to Jane, who had remained in the room as she knew she would be needed. What he said, I don't know, but Jane took me outside, shut the door, and stated, "I will help Sarah get washed up and fed while the five of them confer. The good Doctor wants you to go down to the conference room and start the chapter editing going and Sir Roger will be down soon."

*   *   *

So, here we are. We won't end this chapter without finding out who Sarah really is and the details of her adventure and what is in those bags. Let us talk about money issues and extended families until our guest baker, Sir Roger, can get away. He knows to come to where I am.

The Fuel for Families: Money

What happened upstairs leads us right to our overall topic for this chapter. We live in a time when the basic individual family now needs both husband and wife to be fully and gainfully employed in order to have what is considered a base standard of living. Emerging and Young Adults now not only want to live better than their parents, make more money, and have a bigger house, but they also want it all now! They do tend to have a lot of money at their disposal but are short on their own experience on what to do with it or manage it.

Money, how much each family has of it, how it is valued, and how individuals go about using it, is very much related to the values and norms of our society today. They all go together with no clear indication which one drives the other e.g. the price of gasoline in America. This price is related to many factors including a strong value of individualism, and an individual ownership of cars, reluctance to put any real money into a national public transportation system. A contributing factor is the capitalistic free enterprise system, propped up by our government's laws that allow speculators to make money on the shorting of sales of oil and related products. In addition, our economic system has given corporations permission to act like individuals on social matters while maintaining huge tax breaks and subsidies for corporations like oil companies and other mega businesses. Yet corporations don't have souls or much in the way of feelings.

Finally, as a society, Americans are used to valuing hard work and the quality of the work or the products we produce, knowing that both those factors would result in our company making a profit. The employer used to value the American worker and support them so that they would be the best in the world. Now the values of the working place are all related to making a profit first, not in producing a valuable and "best it can be" product. The American worker has been propagandized into being an evil force rather than the hero of the working system. Now days it is the CEO who is the hero and s(he) is king/queen as far as making as much money as s(he) can. I would rewrite starting with companies have no loyalty anymore . . . There is not loyalty to their workingforce by companies any more nor is there any loyalty from the worker back to his/her company. All these factors either reflect the values of our society or have highly influenced our country's values; I am not sure which way it works.

*　*　*

And More to Come

There is a knock on the door and Sir Roger and Kelly come in. Dr. D. and the Barristers have not yet returned. They most likely stayed back with the Barristers. Sir Roger sees the questioning look on my face and volunteers: "Yes, we know the rest of Sarah's story. It is true that those big grocery bags were stuffed full of fifty and one hundred dollar bills. How many, I can't even guess but she is carrying around a lot of money. When we heard the rest of her story, I told Dr. D. what I would recommend to Sarah and her eyes lit up. The Barristers liked my idea as well, so they are with Sarah implementing it. I'll let one of them, or perhaps Sarah herself, tell you where she goes from here and how she gets the money to its final destination. For now, let's talk with the readers about families and money. Kelly will lead and I will stay with her and you can go on, or if you like, go find Aunt Sarah and help her get it all cleared up."

*　*　*

Can you imagine how much money there is in two grocery bags full of fifty and one hundred dollar bills?

To find out, a password is needed. The remaining portion of the chapter may be found on the website www.TheFamilyForever. info. When you own the book, read the story of Uncle Charlie and learn the major sport that Uncle Charlie played and how he got into so much trouble. Take the name of that sport and go to www. TheFamilyForever.info.

On that site is the remainder of this bonus chapter, over a dozen pages. Go to "The Vault" and swing open the big door. When you are told that you can go no further because the "page is password protected," type in that single word (all lower case letters) that lists Uncle Charlie's sport and you will be given access to the entire chapter. You may read it there or print it or just download to a flash drive for your later use.

On the bonus site, read what Sir Roger has to say about: (1) how we have given our parenting opportunity and responsibility away and how we can get it back; (2) what are value basics for our college-bond offspring about the use of money beyond how to use your checkbook; (3) if the answer is yes, what are some key steps in the learning experience so that they learn something; (4) if the answer is no, how will you deal with the emotional pressure and storm that is likely to follow; (5) what is suggested that you do as a parent of an adult child in helping them comprehend and manage their financial lives in the economy we presently face; (6) when is having a financial advisor a good idea for a young adult; and (7) what is a financial legacy"

Hope to see you back here very soon.

© 2013 Dr. D.'s Domains

Appendix

The book *Families are Forever: Communication* is the first book in the trilogy. It focuses on the communication ways and patterns of normal, healthy American families. The goal is to help people experience the best that a family can offer them. The book describes the extended family of the 21st century and provides recipes on what you might do to have the best family experience. The eBook version is being published by AuthorHouse publishing and can be ordered for $4.95 from their website: www.AuthorHouse.com/Bookstore. The paperback version is being published by SBPRA Publishing. Both are available through all the normal distributors such as Amazon, Barnes and Noble, Apple and from my website at www.theFamilyForever.com. An mid- September publishing date is anticipated.

The book *Families are Forever: Feelings, Those Rascals*, is the second book in the trilogy. My wife Nancy Cogswell, R.N., is the co-author of this book, a role she carried our extremely well unofficially for the other book. This book deals with the complex world of emotions and feelings. It starts with those common in everyday family relationships, examining how they are caused and what one can do to reduce or eliminate bad feelings. The book ends with a focus on feelings in mature relationships of parents of adult children and how they change and can be enhanced. The final chapters of this book deal with intimate feelings and intimate relationships of all types. Description and recipes to help one have the best feeling experience are offered. No publication contract has been sought at this time for either an eBook or printed version. A 2014 publication date is anticipated.

Free, sample chapters from this book are presently available in the Dr. D's Books section of www.thefamilyforever.com. The projected Table of Contents for Book Two is as follows:

Families are Forever:

Those Rascal Feelings!

Dr. Dennis and Nancy Cogswell

Table of Contents

More Than Expected. Bonus Chapter for Those Who Buy the Book. Located via password on webpages at www.theFamilyForever.info

The book **Families are Forever: Family Relationships** is the third book in the trilogy. This book looks at all types of extended family relationships including traditional and non-traditional family types.

Special chapters on Boomerang families, families with divorced or separated parents, families with teenagers, and extended families that are beginning to add grandchildren are offered. The situations we all face in terms of relationship hurdles in our families are addressed and ways to move forever and over those hurdles are offered. No publication contract has been sought at this time for either an eBook or printed version. A late 2014 publication date is projected. Much of this book is being written now.

Free, sample chapters from this book are presently available in the Dr. D's Books section of www.thefamilyforever.com. The present Table of Contents for this book is as follows:

Families are Forever: Family Relationships

Table of Contents

1. The Relationship(s)
2. The Conflict Quandary: Judging, Forgivingness or Reconciliation
3. The Feuding Family Fable
4. The Apple That Falls Near the Tree: Parent and Adult Child Relationships
5. The Apple That Falls Far From the Tree: Parent and Adult Child Relationships
6. Becoming a Woman: A Woman's View
7. Becoming a Man: A Man's View
8. The Boomerangers
9. Empty Nesting It: Making Now Good Like Then® We're
10. Having a Baby!! The Grandparents Exclaim. Sliding
11. From Independence to Interdependence and Back New
12. Beginnings and Old Hurts
13. Life's Journey: From Doing to Being
14. Professionals Who Work With Families. **Bonus Chapter for Those Purchasing the Book. Located via password on webpages at** www.thefamilyforever.info

A separate, yet supporting book: **Families are Forever: Quotes and Notes from the Good Doctor** is planned for the 2013-2015 time periods. It will focus on quotes from famous people along with quotes from Dr. Cogswell. Each quote will have several paragraphs of commentary pertaining to how those quotes apply to life in present 21th Century American Families. Free, sample pages from this book are presently available in the Kelly's Korner, The Deli, section of www.theFamilyForever.com. The present Table of Contents for this book is as follows:

Families are Forever!
Book Four

Quotes and Notes From the Good Doctor.
Possible Chapters

1. Emotions and Feelings

2. Values

3. Relationships

4. Family Relationships

5. Relationships With the World.

6. Grand parenting

7. Golf Rules for Life I

8. Golf Rules for Life II

9. -13 TBA

* * *

PODCASTS. Audio recordings known as podcasts for Every chapter of every book will become available for free at our website and at the ITunes store soon after the publication date. See www.TheFamilyForever.com for full information.

Person interested in playing the world's only underground golf course, viewing famous videos at The Screening Section, or looking through the Hubble Observatory telescope, viewing many resources pertaining to being an author, gathering family recipes at Nana's Nook and reading in an extensive library pertaining to families and family counseling at our University Hall may do so at www.theFamilyForever.com.

Those interested in commentary pertaining to families and posting responses may do so via www.theFamilyForever.Wordpress.com.

Our newest and oldest family member, three hundred and ninety-three year old Squire Bin Forever, hailing from Westbury Leigh, England and Williamsburg, Virginia has just joined the Forever Family. He is the key speaker at many of our family's speaking functions and even has his own website at www. SquireBin.Forever.com. Come and visit him there. His motto is: "New to you but not to the World."

Squire Bin Forever
Contact Information may be found at www.SquireBinForever.com

Works Cited

Becvar & Becvar. (1999) *Systems theory and family therapy. A primer*. Washington, D.C. University Press of America, p. 103.

Burns, D. (1992/1980). *Feeling Good: The New Mood Therapy*. New York: Avon Books.

Campbell, J. (1988). *An Open Life*. New York: Harper and Row.

Cogswell, D. (2013). *The Forever Family: Library Resources*. Retrieved March 2013, from http://www.thefamilyforever.com/the-library-hbse-resources.html

Cogswell, D. D. (2013). *Tick Tock: The Clock Rules!* In D. D. Cogswell, *Families are Forever: Communication.*

Cogswell, D. (2012). *Notes and Quotes of the Good Doctor* (written but presently unpuplished).

Gulley, P. (2010). *If the Church Were Christian: Rediscovering the Values of Jesus.* New York: Harper One.

http://www.classicrotaryphones.com/advertisements4.html

http://en.wikipedia.org/wiki/Gone_with_the_Wind

http://en.wikipedia.org/wiki/Mary_Poppins_(musical)

http://shareranks.com/9097,Best-California-Wines-Under-$20#b#ixzz2IaaXkEwl

http://www. BearleyBear.com

http://www.cdc.gov/immunizations

http://www.SquireBinForever.com

http://www.theadultchild.com/relationships-and-time-structuring-a-typology.html

http://www.thefamilyforever.com

http://www.thefamilyforever.info

James, M. &. Joungward, D. (1996). *Born to Win: Twenty-fifth Anniversary Issue*. *New York:* Addison—Wesley Publishing.

Lencioni, P. (2002). *The Five Dysfunctions of a Team: A Leadership Fable*. San Francisco: Jossey-Bass.

Micheal McCullough et ale, K. P. (2000). *Forgiveness: Theory, Research and Practice.* New York: Gillford Press.

Minuchin, S. a. (1993). *Family Healing: Strategies for Hope and Understanding*. New York: The Free Press.

Mitchell, M. (1939). Retrieved October 26th, 2012, from Nichols, M. (2006*). Family Therapy: Concepts and Methods (Seventh Edition).* Boston: Pearson Education.

Rohr, R. (2012). *Preparing for Christmas*. Cincinnati, Ohio: Franciscan Media.

Tanner, J. e. (2001). *Emerging adulthood: Learning and development during the first stage of adult hood.* Retrieved January 2013, from http://www.rci.rutgers.edu/tmusner/tammer.%20 Arnett%20leischapter%202%in%20Smith%520Handbook.pdf

Tolle, E. (n.d.). *Wikapedia, the free encyercolpedia.* Retrieved October 26th, 2012, from http://en.wikipedia.org/wiki/ Eckhart_Tolle.

U.S. Census Bureau. (20101) Retrieved from www.census.gov: www.census.gov

Youtube.com/watch?v=EyG12LxME

Wikapedia, the free encylocpedia. Retrieved October 26th, 2012, from Wikapedia: http://en.wikipedia.org/wiki/Human_behavior

Wikapedia, the free encylocpedia. (date unknown). Retrieved 2012, from Wikapedia: http://en.wikipedia.org/wiki/Cognition.

Wikipedia.org/wiki/Social_sciences. Wilkpedia. Retrieved from en.wikipedia.org/wiki/Social_sciences

Other Recommended Sources

Ahrons, C. (2004). *We're Still Family. What Grown Children Have to Say About Their Parents' Divorce.* New York: Harper

Albom, A. (1997). *Tuesdays with Morrie.* New York: Broadway Books.

Barkley R., and Benton, C. (1998) *Your Defiant Child: Eight Steps to Better Behavior.* New York: Guilford.

Becvar, D. & Becvar, R. (2003). *Family Therapy: A Systemic Integration (Fifth Edition).* Boston: Pearson Education.

Berne, E. (1971). *Games People Play: The Psychology of Human Relationships.* New York: Castle Books.

Bluestein, J. (1993). *Parents, Teens and Boundaries: How to Draw the Line.* Deerfield Beach, FL: Health Communications.

Bottke, Allison (2008). *Setting Boundaries with Your Adult Children: Six Steps to Hope and Healing for Struggling Parents.* Eugene, Oregon, Harvest House Publishers.

Bower, S & Bower, G. (1991). *Asserting Yourself: A Practical Guide for Positive Change.* Reading, Massachusetts" Pereus Books.

Brown, E. (1999). *Living Successfully With Screwed-Up People.* Grand Rapids, Michigan: Revell.

Burns, D. (1980). *Feeling Good: The New Mood Therapy.* New York: Avon Books.

Campbell, J. and Moyers, B. (1988). *The Power of Myth.* New York: Anchor Books.

Campbell, Ross and Chapman, Gary (1999*). Parenting Your Adult Child: How You Can Help Them Achieve Their Full Potential.* Chicago: Northfield Publishing.

Coleman, Joshua. (2008). *When Parents Hurt: Compassionate Strategies When You and Your Grown Child Don't Get Along.* New York: HarperCollins Publisher.

Cooper, D. (1997). *God is a Verb: Kabbalah and the Practice of Mystical Judaism.* New York: Riverhead Books.

Covey, S. (1997). *The 7 Habits of Highly Effective Families: Building a Beautiful Culture in a Turbulent World.* New York: Golden Books.

Dalbey, G. (2011). *Sons of the Father: Healing the Father Wound in Men Today.* Folsome, California: CivitasPress.

Dattilo, F. & Jongsma, Jr., A. (2000). *The Family Therapy Treatment Planner.* New York: John Wiley and Sons.

Davies, P. (1983). *God and the New Physics.* New York: Touchstone.

Davies, P. (1995). *About Time: Einstein's Unfinished Revolution.* New York: Touchstone.

Diamond, M. (2007) *My Father Before Me: How Fathers and Sons Influence Each Other Throughout Their Lives.* New York: W.W. Norton & Company.

Dossey, L. (1997). *Healing Words: The Power of Prayer and the Practice of Medicine.* New York: Harper Collins.

Forehand R. and Long, N. (1996). *Parenting the Strong-Willed Child*. Chicago: Contemporary Books.

Fuller, C. & Plum, Ali. (2010). *Mother-Daughter Duet: Getting the Relationship You Want with Your Adult Daughter*. Colorado Springs, Colorado: Multnomah Books.

Gilbert, R. (1992**).** *Extraordinary Relationships: A New Way of Thinking*. Minneapolis: Chronimed Publishing.

Gottlieb, G. (2006). *Letters to Sam: A Grandfather's Lessons on Love, Loss, and the Gifts of Life.* New York: Sterling Publishing Company, Inc.

Greenspan, S. (1995). *The Challenging Child.* Reading, MA: Perseus Books.

Hasslet, C. (2008). *20 Something Manifesto: Quarter-Lifers Speak Out About Who They Are, What They Want, and How to Get It.* Novato, California: New World Library.

Hepworth, D., Rooney, R., & Larsen, J. (1997). *Direct Social Work Practice; Theory and Skills (Fifth Edition).* Pacific Grove, California: Brooks/Cole Publishing Company.

Herst, C. and Padwa, L.(1999). *For Mothers of Difficult Daughters: How to Enrich and Repair the Relationship in Adulthood*. New York: Villard.

Hutchison, E & Contributors. (2011). *Dimensions of Human Behavior: The Changing life Course (Fourth Edition).* Thousand Oaks, California: Sage.

Isay, Jane. (2007). *Walking on Eggshells: Navigating the Delicate Relationship Between Adult Children and Parents.* New York: Flying Dolphin Press, Broadway Books.

James, M & Joungward, D. (2000). *Born to Win: Transactional Analysis with Gestalt Experiments.* Reading, Massachusetts: Addison-Wesley Publishing Company.

Johnson, R. (2006). *Better Dads, Stronger Sons: How Fathers Can Guide Boys to Become Men of Character.* Grand Rapids, Michigan: Revell.

Kilpatrick, A & Holldan, T. (2009). *Working With Families: An Integrative Model by Level of Need (Fifth Edition).* Boston: Pearson.

King, M. (2010). *Strength to Love.* Minneapolis: Fortress Press.

Lencioni, P. (2002). *The Five Dysfunctions of a Team: A Leadership Fable*. San Francisco: Jossey-Bass.

Libby, B. (1992). *The Forgiveness Book*. Boston: Cowley Publications.

McCullough, M., Pargament, K & Thoresen, C. (2000). *Forgiveness: Theory, Research and Practice.* New York: The Guilford Press.

McGoldrick, M. (1995). *You Can Go Home Again: Reconnecting With Your Family*. New York: W.W. Norton and Company.

McGraw, Phil. (1999*). Life Strategies: Doing What Works/Doing What Matters.* New York: Hyperion.

Medea, A. (2006*). Going Home Without Going Crazy: How to Get Along with Your Parents & Family, Even When They Push Your Buttons.* Oakland, California: New Harbinger Publications. Inc.

Minuchin, S. and Nichols, M (1998) *Family Healing: Strategies for Hope and Understanding*. New York: The Free Press

Mitchell, S (1996). *Genesis: A New Translation of the Classical Biblical Stories.* New York: Harper Collins.

Napier, A. (1978). *The Family Crucible: The Intense Experience of Family Therapy.* New York: Harper and Row.

Nemzoff, Ruth. (2008). *Don't Bite Your Tongue: How to Foster Rewarding Relationships with Your Adult Children.* New York: Palgrave MacMillian.

Nepo, M. (2011). *The Book of Awakening: Having the Life You Want by Being Present to the Life You Have.* San Francisco: Conari Press.

Nichols, M. and Schwarta, R. (2006). *Family Therapy: Concepts and Methods (Seventh Edition).* Boston: Pearson.

Olson, D. and DeFrain (2003) *Marriage and Families: Intimacy, Diversity and Strengths.* New York: McGraw-Hill.

Parent, Gail and Ende, S. (2010). *How to Raise Your Adult Children: Because Big Kids Have Even Bigger Problems.* New York: Hudson Street Press.

Peck, M. (1997). *The Road Less Traveled and Beyond.* New York: Simon and Schuster.

Pipher, M. (1996). *The Shelter of Each Other: Rebuilding Our Families*. New York: G.P. Putnam's Sons.

Remen, R. (2000). *My Grandfather's Blessings: Stories of Strength, Refuse, and Belonging.* New York: Riverhead Books.

Robbins, A. and Wilner, A. (2001). *Quarterlife Crisis: The Unique Challenges of Life in Your Twenties.* New York: Putnam.

Rohr, Richard. (2003). *Everything Belongs: The Gift of Contemplative Prayer.* New York: The Crossroad Publishing Company.

Settersten, Richard and Ray, Barbara. (2010). *Not Quite Adults: Why 20-Somethings Are Chosing a Slower Path to Adulthood and Why It's Good for Everyone*. New York: Bantam Dell.

Shaputis, K. (2003). *The Crowded Nest Syndrome: Surviving the Return of Adult Children.* Olympia, Washington: Clutster Fairy Publishing.

Warren, R. (2002). *The Purpose Driven Life: What On Earth Am I Here For?* Grand Rapids, Michigan; Zondervan.

Watsch, N. (1996-2006). *Conversations With God" An Uncommon Dialogue (Eight Books)*. New York: G.P. Putnam's Sons.

Watsh, F. (Editor). (1999). *Spirtuality Resources in Family Therapy*. New York: The Guildford Press.

Willaimson, M (1992). *A Return to Love: Reflections on the Principles of a Course in Miracles.* New York: Harper Collins.

Subject and Name Index

Y

Related Photos

Dennis and Nancy Cogswell
who write as themselves and as Dr. D. and Nana.

Dennis Cogswell, as Dr. D; writing the book outdoors.

Kristen, Drew and Lauren Cogswell
They Make Us an Extended Family.

Charles "Hobs" Hobgood
Key family consultant, guest author, and family philosopher

Squire Bin Forever, Age 293

"New to You But Not to the World"
Forever Family Spokesperson
www.SquireBinForever.com

Bearley Bear
Speaks Multiple Languages
Children's Books Spokesbear.
Hugging is Closeness
www.BearleyBear.com

Thefamilyforever

Families Forever Mobius Logo

Dr.o•s Domains
More Than Expected